SPIRIT OF BERMUDA
COOKING WITH GOSLING'S BLACK SEAL RUM®

BY EDWARD BOTTONE

Illustrated by Joanne Radmilovich

Art Direction & Design by Paul Shapiro

THE BERMUDIAN PUBLISHING COMPANY LIMITED

Published by The Bermudian Publishing Company Limited,
P.O. Box HM 283, Hamilton HM AX, Bermuda

Book and cover design by Paul Shapiro, Brimstone Media

First edition

ISBN 976-8143-25-8

Printed in Singapore

Introduction

The Bermuda Bar

Soups & Starters

Main Courses

Sides, Salads & Sandwiches

Cooking Outdoors

Contents

Holiday Traditions

Desserts

*Dedicated to Bermuda, and to Charles Gosling
and the Gosling family's generosity of spirit*

Spirit of Bermuda

Ever since Queen Elizabeth's favourite admiral, Sir George Somers, shipwrecked off the Island, the spirit of Bermuda has been alive and well.

In the Age of Discovery, the New World was an irresistible destination. The stalwart sailors and adventurers on board the *Sea Venture* had set out on a rescue mission bound to save the starving colony at Jamestown, America's first British settlement.

Although the *Sea Venture* was wrecked on East End reefs (today called Sea Venture Shoals), its destination was, and remained, Jamestown, Virginia. A new ship, the *Deliverance*, was built from salvaged pieces of the broken ship. Another vessel, made entirely of Bermuda cedar, the *Patience*, was also constructed for the voyage.

The following spring, they set out to save the Jamestown colony. Edward Chard, Robert Waters and Christopher Carter stayed behind and would not see another soul for two long years.

In 1612, the *Plough* arrived with 50 settlers, and the great struggle to survive and flourish began. The Spanish, French and Portuguese all had come before them, but none had remained on the Island. These were the earliest Bermudians (there were no indigenous people), and from the start, these settlers had the spirit of Bermuda.

Time and again, this spirit is what sustained Bermuda. The spirit to survive, to thrive and prosper on one of the most isolated, beautiful spots in the world—650 nautical miles from landfall.

Bermudians have, over the years, farmed for survival, raked salt, were pirates and privateers, master ship-builders, whalers and export farmers. So prodigious were they with arrow-root, the Easter lily and sweet onion, that these became synonymous with the Island. They were blockade-runners during America's Civil War and rum-runners during Prohibition; soldiers of fortune and fortunate soldiers, merchants and hosts. In the 17th century, they triumphed over famine, rat infestation, sectarianism and witch-craft. In the 18th century, they survived divisions of allegiance between the revolutionaries in America and the Crown. They were Britain's Gibraltar of the West and saw the attack on America's capital launched from Bermuda in 1814. They built the finest ships under sail, until the advent of steam. Later, with no natural resources but their own resourcefulness, they prospered in the industrial age, even though Bermuda had no industry.

They recognised their Island was their industry, and practically invented Island tourism. They had the spirit. Some of the wonders of the age came to Bermuda with startling promptness: the first telephone in 1882, the first trans-atlantic cable system, set up by Cable & Wireless in 1890, the first electric light in 1908, a railway in 1931, the first commercial airflight in 1937. Others came mercifully late: cars were first permitted in 1947, and television came to the Island in 1958. Always Bermudians had the spirit. Every time it seemed they had exhausted their options they looked to Bermuda and it renewed their spirit, fortified their independence, strength-ened their will.

Today, Bermuda is one of the world's leading tourist destinations and a centre for international business. What would Sir George say?

RUM & THE GOSLING FAMILY

Just less than 200 years after the wreck of the *Sea Venture*, serendipity also brought James Gosling to Bermuda. In the spring of 1806, James, the oldest son of wine and spirits merchant William Gosling, set out from England on the ship *Mercury* with £10,000 of merchandise, bound for America.

After 91 desperate days on a becalmed sea, their charter ran out and they were forced to put in at the nearest port—St. George's, Bermuda. Rather than pressing on for America, James opened a shop on the King's Parade, St. George's, in December, 1806.

By 1824, James had returned to England and his brother Ambrose, who had joined him earlier in Bermuda, opened Ambrose Gosling and Sons on Front Street, in the new capital of Hamilton. The Goslings maintained a store at this location for 127 years.

In 1857, the firm was renamed Gosling Brothers by Ambrose's sons. Three years later, the first oak barrels of rum distillate arrived in Bermuda. After much experimentation, the distinctive Bermuda black rum, destined to become Gosling's Black Seal Rum®, was formulated and offered for sale. Until the First World War, it was sold from the barrel, and most folks brought in their own bottles for a fill-up of "old rum," as they called the potent, mellow spirit.

Eventually the black rum was sold in champagne bottles, reclaimed from the British officers' mess, corked and sealed with black wax. Pretty soon, people began to ask for the "Black Seal." Many years later, the play on words and images gave birth to the cute, barrel-juggling black seal. Today there's a shop on Front Street celebrating Gosling's Black Seal Rum, and its mascot, which appears on everything from hats to boxer shorts.

Over the years, Gosling's Black Seal Rum has become synonymous with Bermuda. An essential additive to local fish chowder, it also adds the Island touch to Bermuda rum swizzles, and is the tempest in Bermuda's favourite cocktail —the Dark 'n Stormy. Gosling's Black Seal Rum, superb neat or over ice, adds uniqueness to many mixed drinks and dishes both savoury and sweet. Recently, Gosling's Black Seal Rum was awarded the platinum medal in the International World Spirits Championships.

A family business for nearly two centuries, Gosling's is Bermuda's oldest business house and is the largest exporter of a Bermuda-made product.

The Bermuda Bar

Equipment

All it takes to set up a Bermuda bar

For most mixed drinks, you'll need a proper shaker. Get a professional one; it's worth the extra money. I prefer one stainless steel shaker, and one made of glass so you can see it all rocking back and forth. Traditionally, you resort to a shaker when you're attempting to combine ingredients not easily blended by simply stirring—things like cream, juices, milk, eggs or heavy syrups. Naturally, you'll require a stainless steel bar strainer, and a long-handled bar spoon. You'll also need a couple of 'shot' glasses (1½-ounce measure).

An electric blender is absolutely essential to the island bar. I suggest a professional model with a glass canister. Have a waiter's corkscrew, a small, good-quality serrated knife for cutting fruit, a nutmeg grater, a small wooden cutting board, and straws—the bright paper umbrellas, plastic mermaids, monkeys and flamingoes are up to you.

Try not to have too many different-sized glasses. You should have some old-fashioned glasses, classic whiskey sour glasses, champagne flutes, highball or tall drink glasses, large tulips for 'exotic' drinks, and heat-proof punch cups. Most drinks will fit nicely and look appealing in at least one of these.

RUM FACTS **What's in a Name?** Rum was once called "rumbullion" because it could cause an uproar, and "kill-devil" because it could drive away the demons of sickness. It was also called "rumbustion" and described by Richard Ligon in 1651 as a "hot, hellish, terrible liquor." And perhaps, in those days it was—raw, fiery, and potent. Rumbullion, rumbustion—is that how it got its name? Perhaps, but some think it came from the latin for the sugar, *saccharum*, from which it's derived. Some say it was a diminutive of the French for aroma, *arome*. But why then do they spell it "rhum"?

Stocking a Bermuda Bar

SPIRITS
Gosling's Black Seal Rum (80-proof/151-proof), Gosling's Rum Deluxe (amber), Gosling's Choicest Barbados Rum, Gosling's Bermuda Light Rum, tequila, gin, vodka, Scotch, Canadian whisky.

LIQUEURS
Bermuda Banana Liqueur, Bermuda Coconut Rum Liqueur, Bermuda Gold, Triple Sec (regular and blue), di Saronno Amaretto, apricot brandy, peach brandy, Drambuie, coffee liqueur, Galliano, Romana Sambuca.

WINES
Champagne, sweet and dry vermouth, port.

JUICES, ETC.
Rose's Lime Juice, fresh lemon and orange juice, unsweetened pineapple juice, tomato juice, mango, papaya and passion fruit juices, coconut cream and milk.

SYRUPS & FLAVOURINGS
Grenadine, falernum (made only in Bermuda and Barbados), Angostura Bitters, orgeat (a syrup of almonds and orange-flower water), green olives, maraschino cherries, Tabasco, Worcestershire sauce, pepper, salt, nutmeg, bar sugar.

MIXERS
Club soda, cola, ginger beer, ginger ale, tonic water.

FRESH FRUIT
Oranges, lemons, limes, mangoes, strawberries, papayas, pineapple, bananas.

THE
BERMUDA
BAR

A NOTE ON ICE You cannot underestimate the importance of ice in an island bar. Island drinks must always be served very cold, except, of course, when they are hot drinks. Strained, stirred drinks should be made in a large pitcher with plenty of ice cubes (not crushed ice, which dilutes the drink). Serving a cold drink in a cold glass enhances the quality of the experience.

Rum Drinks & Other 'Re-frashments'

Rum Swizzle

Our national drink. Everyone has at least one, which leads to another. Traditionally these are frothed with a Bermuda swizzle stick. Literally, a stick that ends in three prongs, often cut from an allspice bush.

6 oz Gosling's Barbados Rum
2–3 oz Gosling's Black Seal Rum
1 oz apricot brandy
juice of 4 ripe limes
1½ oz Bermuda falernum (or simple syrup)
Angostura Bitters to taste
orange slices and maraschino cherries for garnish

Fill a pitcher a third full with ice cubes. Add all of the above and churn vigorously with a swizzle stick until a bit of 'sea foam' appears on the top. Strain into sour glasses, garnish with a cherry toothpicked to a slice of orange.

Some of these recipes are for a single serving, some for a few thirsty souls and others for a whole lot of libation.

THE
BERMUDA
BAR

Dark 'n Stormy

Our other national drink had its origins in the highly successful ginger beer factory, run as a subsidiary to the Royal Navy officers' club. Members soon discovered a splash of local black rum was just what the ginger beer was missing. The name was said to have originated when an old salt, holding aloft the thunderhead in a glass, observed the drink was the "colour of a cloud only a fool or dead man would sail under." Probably followed by, "Barman, I'll have another Dark 'n Stormy."

Simply add Gosling's Black Seal Rum to chilled ginger beer according to your taste and tolerance. Serve on the rocks.

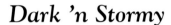

Bermuda's First Toast

Rum was well known to Sir George Somers, who, when he came aground on Bermuda at St. Catherine's Point in 1609, shared a celebratory dram of "comfortable waters," that is to say rum, with the other survivors.

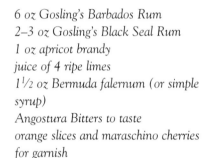

Bermuda Shrub

Derived from the Arabic *shurb*, meaning a draught or drink. In the 19th century in the US, it was a name given to a cordial derived from raspberries, vinegar and sugar.

1 gallon Gosling's Rum Deluxe
3 pints boiling water
6 lb dark brown sugar
3 pints juice of sour Bermuda oranges
2–3 tbs ginger, grated
1 nutmeg, grated

Dissolve half the sugar in the rum. Add the spices and stir well. Bring to a boil for 10 minutes. Boil the remaining three pounds of sugar with the water for 10–15 minutes. Mix all together and let cool, then stand in a cool place for at least 10 days. Strain through a double layer of cheesecloth and transfer to bottles. Makes a nice gift. Mixed with boiling water, it's excellent for soothing a sore throat.

THE
BERMUDA
BAR

13

Black Seal Sour

juice of half a lemon
juice of half a ripe lime
1 tsp bar sugar
dash Angostura Bitters
2 oz Gosling's Black Seal Rum

Shake ingredients to a froth. Strain into a sour glass and decorate with maraschino cherry and a lime slice.

Gosling's Goose

In a tall glass filled with ice, combine:

2 oz Gosling's Black Seal Rum
6 oz fresh orange juice

The Islander

In a tall glass filled with ice, combine:

2 oz Gosling's Black Seal Rum
6 oz fresh pineapple juice

THE
BERMUDA
BAR

The Bermuda Angler

Created in the 1930s by E.F. Warner, then-publisher of *Field and Stream*.

2 oz Gosling's Barbados Rum
1 oz fresh lime juice
1 tsp Triple Sec

Shake all together with ice and strain into a cocktail glass.

Between the Sheets

1/2 oz Gosling's Bermuda Light Rum
1/2 oz brandy
1/2 oz fresh lemon juice
1/2 oz curaçao

Shake together with ice and strain into a cocktail glass.

Charles' Fruit Punch

1/2 cup Gosling's Rum Deluxe
1/2 cup Gosling's Black Seal Rum
3 cups passion fruit juice
1 cup guava juice
1 cup pineapple juice
1 cup orange juice
Angostura Bitters to taste

Mix the rums, juices, and bitters in a large ice-filled pitcher and stir vigorously. Serve in tumblers, with or without rocks.

Loquat Liqueur

Gather ye loquats while ye may, in February and March. Then make this aromatic concoction which should be perfect by the fall of the year. This traditional potion was the origin of Bermuda Gold Liqueur, made by Somers Distillers.

3 lbs dead ripe loquats—snip off the pointed ends, leave in stones

2 lbs rock crystal candy
gallon of Gosling's Bermuda Light Rum

In a gallon jug, put alternating layers of loquats and rock crystal candy until all are used up. Fill the jug to the top with rum. Seal well, then seal the seal with aluminum foil. Let stand in a cool, dark place, turning it upside down, and then down side up, every 2 weeks. In about 2 months, most of the sugar will have dissolved and a tawny gold liqueur will remain. Leave the jug until the beginning of August. At that time, strain the velvety liqueur through a double layer of cheesecloth, removing any fruit and imperfections. You have not, however, reached the time of golden reward.

Allow the strained liqueur to age until late October. Your first sip should justify the long wait. The colour of gold, a divine perfume and velvety smoothness should make the moment memorable. Invite friends for a sip. Also makes a perfect fruit sour cocktail, is delicious over ice-cream, and is used in an elegant dessert—Bermuda Gold Peaches (see Page 125).

Planter's Punch

3 tbs fresh lime juice
3 tbs fresh lemon juice
³⁄4 cup orange juice
³⁄4 cup pineapple juice
1¹⁄2 oz Bermuda falernum (or simple syrup)
¹⁄2 cup Gosling's Black Seal Rum
¹⁄2 cup Gosling's Rum Deluxe
orange slices, cherries and umbrellas for garnish

THE
BERMUDA
BAR

GOING FOR GOLD

It wasn't long after the loquat was introduced to Bermuda in the 1840s that locals started making smooth, amber loquat liqueur. In those days, it was considered a sipping drink suitable for afternoon tea.

In the mid-1960s, having already begun commercial production of sherry peppers, Yeaton Outerbridge and John Profit decided to make a loquat cordial for general consumption. They sampled home brews made from the little golden fruit, rock sugar and gin or vodka and set about making their own in the slave quarters of 300-year-old Villa Monticello. Three years later, they formed Somers Distributors, named after Sir George, and launched 'Bermuda Gold.' Emblazoned with the ill-fated ship, *Sea Venture*, 4,000 bottles sold the first year. Today, Somers Distillers, a subsidiary of Gosling Brothers, sells the liqueur to aficionados at home and abroad. It's delicious for sipping, as a cocktail, and superb for poaching pears (Page 123) or making a sauce for duck (Page 52).

You can mix the juices and falernum ahead of time and chill. When ready to serve, mix the juices and rums in a pitcher filled with ice and stir vigorously. Serve in tumblers, ridiculously garnished, with or without rocks.

Roun' de Verld

In days of yore, folks would come brandishing their own bottles to the Gosling's shop to eye the various barrels of wines and spirits. They'd ask for a "round the world"—a little from each. This recipe is a homage to those days.

1 oz Gosling's Black Seal Rum
1 oz gin
1 oz whiskey
1 oz port

Shake together with plenty of ice and strain into a tall glass. Whew!

Bermuda Iced Tea

$^1\!/_2$ oz Gosling's Black Seal Rum
$^1\!/_2$ oz vodka
$^1\!/_2$ oz gin
$^1\!/_2$ oz Triple Sec
$^1\!/_2$ oz orange juice
cola

Shake with ice, top with a splash of cola and a squeeze of lemon. Looks and tastes like iced tea. Different effect, though.

THE
BERMUDA
BAR

Black 'n Coke

2 oz Gosling's Black Seal Rum
6 oz Coca-Cola
juice of half a lime

Mix together in a glass filled with ice.

Peachy Mai Tai

1 oz De Kuyper Peachtree
1 oz Gosling's Black Seal Rum
juice of half a fresh lime
lime wedge, maraschino cherry for garnish

Place all ingredients in a blender with ice and blend until smooth. Pour into a goblet and decorate with a wedge of lime and maraschino cherry.

Surf's Up

1 oz Gosling's Bermuda Light Rum
1 oz Southern Comfort
1 oz Bermuda Banana Liqueur
2 oz peach brandy
1 oz fresh orange juice
1 dash of grenadine
toasted coconut for garnish

Blend the first 6 ingredients with ice until smooth. Pour into a large goblet and decorate with toasted coconut. A spoon may be necessary. If you've a flair for the dramatic, serve in halved coconut shells with all but a

¼-inch of the coconut meat removed.

Classic Daiquiri

In 1896, Jennings Cox had a dilemma. The manager of the Spanish-American Iron Co. at Daiquiri Beach near Santiago, Cuba, had thirsty guests and no gin. With what was on hand, he devised this simple refresher. The first mention of the daiquiri is in F. Scott Fitzgerald's *This Side of Paradise*.

3 oz Gosling's Bermuda Light Rum
1 oz fresh lime juice
1 tsp superfine sugar

Shake with ice and strain into cocktail glass. Garnish with a slice of lime.

Classic Frozen Daiquiri

Blend with 2 cups of ice:

2 oz Gosling's Bermuda Light Rum
1 oz fresh lime juice
1 oz Triple Sec
1 tbs bar sugar
garnish with a slice of lime

Variations:

Strawberry: Add 12 fresh strawberries, or a ½ package of frozen (unthawed), to the recipe above and substitute straw-

berry liqueur for the Triple Sec.
Banana: 1 large or 2 medium bananas; substitute banana liqueur for Triple Sec.

Any fresh or frozen fruit may be used—match it up with its liqueur counterpart. Be imaginative!

Manganana Daiquiri

FOR 4

After two of these, you should be able to pronounce its name perfectly.

1 banana, peeled
1 large mango, peeled, pitted
½ cup Gosling's Choicest Barbados Rum
¼ cup superfine sugar
2 tbs fresh lime juice
1 tray of ice cubes
red or green maraschino cherries for garnish

Combine all ingredients in the blender (except the cherries) and let it rip. Blend until smooth. Serve in stemmed or highball glasses. Garnish with a cherry.

Watermelon Daiquiri

4 cups watermelon, seeded and cubed
¼ cup fresh lime juice
¾ cup Gosling's Choicest Barbados Rum
1 rounded tbs of superfine sugar
lime wedges or slices for garnish

Put the cubes of watermelon in a sealed

THE
BERMUDA
BAR

plastic bag and freeze overnight. Dissolve the sugar in the lime juice and rum. Put in the blender, add the frozen watermelon and blend until smooth and slushy. Serve in balloon glasses, or old-time, dish-shaped champagne glasses decorated with a lime wedge.

Piña Colada

2 cups pineapple juice
3/4 cup Coco Lopez coconut cream
1 cup Gosling's Black Seal Rum
3 cups crushed ice
pineapple spears for garnish

Blend together all but the pineapple spears until slushy and serve in frosted tumblers. A tiny umbrella wouldn't hurt this tacky, but tasty, standby. Not surprisingly, this drink, with a teaspoon of vanilla extract substituted for rum, goes over well with kids.

Capri Colada

3/4 oz heavy cream
1/4 oz Coco Lopez coconut cream
2 oz pineapple juice
1/2 cup di Saronno Amaretto
1 oz Gosling's Bermuda Light Rum

Put all ingredients in the blender with a generous scoop of ice and process until slushy. Okay, let's dance!

Yellow Bird

juice of a lime
1 1/2 oz orange juice
1/4 oz Galliano
1 oz Gosling's Bermuda Light Rum
1 oz Gosling's Rum Deluxe
maraschino cherries, mint leaves for garnish

Put all ingredients into a handsome shaker filled with ice and shake vigorously. Strain into a highball glass half filled with crushed ice. Garnish with a cherry and mint sprig.

Zombie

juice of a lemon
3/4 oz orange juice (preferably blood oranges)
3/4 oz grenadine

The Yardarm

'Lighting up time'—read cocktail hour—begins in Bermuda when "the sun crosses the yardarm."

1 oz Gosling's Bermuda Light Rum
1 oz Triple Sec
3 oz grapefruit juice

Shake together all of the ingredients and strain into a highball glass filled with ice.

Christmas Rum Punch (Cold)

juice of 4 oranges
juice of 4 lemons
a whole pineapple, diced (save the juice)
½ cup superfine sugar
¼ cup orange curaçao
1 small bottle maraschino cherries
1 bottle Gosling's Black Seal Rum
1 bottle club soda, chilled
1 orange, sliced for garnish
2 lemons, sliced for garnish

¾ oz Cherry Herring
¾ oz Gosling's Bermuda Light Rum
3 oz Gosling's Black Seal Rum
cherries for garnish

Shake all ingredients with crushed ice. Strain into a highball glass, or a funky Tiki mug, half filled with ice. Garnish with a cherry.

Blue Lagoon

1 oz Bermuda Coconut Rum
½ oz gin
½ oz blue curaçao

Shake all ingredients with ice and serve in champagne 'dish.'

Put the fruit juices, the pineapple with its juice, the cherries along with the liquid from the jar, and the sugar, in a punch bowl and mix well. Add the curaçao and rum and chill well. Just before serving, add the club soda, sliced fruit garnishes and a hunk of ice to keep it all cold. This punch is equally delightful at other festive occasions throughout the year.

Black Seal Manhattan

2 oz Gosling's Black Seal Rum
$^1/_2$ oz sweet vermouth
twist of lime

Stir together with ice, strain into a Manhattan glass, garnish with a cherry.

Bermuda Bloody Mary Deluxe

Dedicated to the memory of Dick Rutherford, founder of Tom Moore's Tavern.

1 oz of vodka
1 oz of gin
8 oz V-8 juice, very cold
several dashes of Tabasco, to taste
hefty squeeze of lemon and lime juice
salt and pepper, to taste
2–3 dashes of Worcestershire sauce
horseradish to taste
dash of celery salt
stick of celery and one lime wedge for garnish

Mix all together with ice and strain into a tall glass and garnish with a celery stalk and lime wedge.

THE
BERMUDA
BAR

Seal-of-Approval Holiday Eggnog

MAKES ABOUT 2 QUARTS

6 eggs, separated
$^1/_2$ cup sugar & $^1/_4$ cup sugar
1 pint heavy whipping cream
1 pint whole milk
6 oz whiskey
4 oz Gosling's Black Seal Rum
2 oz di Saronno Amaretto
freshly grated nutmeg

Beat the yolks with a $^1/_2$ cup sugar until thickened. Beat the whites with a $^1/_4$ cup of sugar until they stand in stiff peaks. Beat the cream until thickened but not whipped hard. Fold together the yolks and whites, then the cream. Add milk to thin. Add whiskey, Gosling's Black Seal Rum and Amaretto. Grate on lots of nutmeg. Chill thoroughly. Put in a large, attractive serving or punch bowl. Garnish each serving with more grated nutmeg.

Café Grog

Grog got its name from grogram cloth, a waxy, stiff fabric used to make weather-proof coats for the Royal Navy. One such coat was the daily uniform of Admiral Edward Vernon, who became known as "Old Grog." It was Old Grog who instituted the practice of diluting the sailors' daily 'tot' of rum to "prevent the ill consequences of stupefying their rational qualities."

2 lumps of sugar
1 oz Gosling's Black Seal Rum
½ oz brandy
coffee to fill
slice of lemon

Dissolve the sugar in the rum and brandy and add very hot coffee and the lemon slice. Enjoy.

Hot Rum Chocolate

1 cup heavy cream
¼ cup chocolate-flavoured liqueur (Godiva Chocolate Mousse is a good one)
3 tbs Gosling's Black Seal Rum
1 square of semi-sweet chocolate to shave on as garnish

Scald cream in a heavy saucepan. Stir in liqueur and Gosling's Black Seal Rum. Pour into two mugs or heat-proof glasses. Garnish with chocolate shavings (use a vegetable peeler).

Spiced Black Rum Cider

1 qt good unfiltered apple cider
1 small orange stuck with 3–4 cloves
1 stick cinnamon
¾ cup apple brandy

¾ cup Gosling's Black Seal Rum
dash of freshly grated nutmeg

Simmer together the cider, orange and cinnamon for 20 minutes. Add the apple brandy and Gosling's Black Seal Rum and bring to heat. Do not boil. Ladle into warm mugs garnished with nutmeg and an orange slice. On cool nights, the perfect defence.

Christmas Rum Punch (Hot)

1 quart fresh orange juice
6–8 peppercorns
½ tsp cinnamon
1 tsp ginger root
½ tsp cloves
½ cup Gosling's Rum Deluxe
½ cup Gosling's Black Seal Rum
½ cup sweet vermouth
sugar

Simmer together the orange juice and the spices for 30 minutes. Do not boil. Add the rums and vermouth and serve. Serve in warmed heat-proof punch cups or mugs into which you have put a ½ teaspoon of sugar.

THE
BERMUDA
BAR

Soups

Bermuda Fish Chowder

FOR 25

As bouillabaisse is to the French and minestrone to the Italians, every fish chowder-maker in Bermuda insists his or her recipe is the most authentic.

A true "chowderhead" will tell you the best fish chowder is made with heads of grouper. Boil 'em up good and pick off all the meat. The head also provides gelatin that helps to thicken the soup. So if you can get 'em, use 'em.

4 qts water
6 rockfish heads (or 3 lbs fillets)
2 tsp vegetable oil
1 lb onions, chopped
1/2 lb peppers, small dice
1/2 lb carrots, small dice
1 lb potatoes, small dice
1 lb leeks, washed, chopped fine
6 ribs celery, chopped
4-oz tin tomato paste
19-oz tin whole tomatoes, seeded, chopped
ground white pepper to taste
2 tsp paprika
1 tsp tarragon
2 tsp curry
2 tsp thyme
salt to taste
2 tsp marjoram
2 tsp oregano
4 cloves garlic, minced
4 bay leaves
1/4 cup Gosling's Black Seal Rum
1/4 cup sherry peppers

Boil rockfish heads in lightly salted water until fully cooked. Remove the heads, set aside to cool. Strain the remaining stock through a fine sieve and set aside. Remove the meat from the bones while still warm. Set aside. Finely chop the vegetables and sauté in vegetable oil until the onions and leeks are translucent. Add the tomato paste and sweat for another 3 minutes. Add the fish stock, fish meat, herbs, spices and chopped tomatoes. Bring to a boil and allow to simmer for at least 2 hours. While the chowder is allowed to cook, be sure to constantly remove any scum or impurities that may rise to the surface. Also during simmering, break up any large pieces of fish that remain. Season with salt, pepper, rum and sherry peppers.

Gosling's Black Seal Rum and sherry peppers should be served on the side so that this dish can be enjoyed to the fullest.

(Thanks to Chef Marcus Wesch)

23

BERMUDIANS ARE ONIONS

For the last century or so, Bermudians have been affectionately known as "Onions." I suppose it's fortunate to be nick-named after a vegetable so universally employed and enjoyed. Imagine being a nation of rutaba-gas! Today the Newport-to-Bermuda yacht race is still called the "Thrash to the Onion Patch."

The onion has been cultivated in Bermuda since at least 1616. By 1762, onions—but not the renowned sweet Bermuda variety—were already an important export.

During the 19th cen-tury, farming languished in favour of shipbuilding. Only 50 acres of onions were under cultivation in 1830, and only two ploughs existed in Bermuda. At the end of the decade, Governor William Reid re-invigorated the interest in agricul-ture, introducing 'modern' farming methods that created an industry.

It was then that the first Açorean Portuguese workers came to Bermuda to farm. They brought with them the mild, sweet, Tenerife variety of onion seed. Our sub-trop-ical climate and rich soil conspired to produce a singular vegetable.

The turnaround was dramatic. More than 330,000 pounds of onions left Bermuda in 1843. Ten years later, the virgin voyage of the Bermuda-built *Pearl* carried 134 barrels and 1,640 baskets filled with Bermuda onions. In 1875, a total of 4,000 tons (or 4.4-million pounds) of onions were exported.

Onions were even used to promote the budding tourism industry. An old Bermuda greeting card cryptically stated: "Blessed is the man who comes to Bermuda (the modern paradise) and is tempted to eat a sweet onion instead of a forbidden apple."

Tiny Bermuda had become an agricultural force to be reckoned with. During the early 1900s, Bermuda was known as a winter play-ground for the well-to-do, as well as the Garden Market of New York City.

SOUPS
AND
STARTERS

RUM FACTS

Buccaneer to Connoisseur

Over the years, rum became synonymous with swashbuckling seafarers and island adventure. Every island cocktail worth its often-poetic name has its beginning in the unmistakable flavour of rum. Gosling's Black Seal Rum, although extraordinary when mixed or as a cooking ingredient, has elevated rum to the sipping level, the choice of the connoisseur.

Bermuda Onion Soup

8–10 Bermuda onions, finely
 chopped
 4 tbs butter
 4 tbs olive oil (or vegetable oil)
 3 tbs flour
 6 cups good chicken broth, hot
 bouquet garni (parsley, thyme, bay
leaf, tied together)
freshly ground white pepper to taste
3 tbs Gosling's Black Seal Rum
3 or more dashes of sherry peppers sauce
toasted, or sautéed rounds of day-old
French bread, topped with Gruyère or
 Swiss cheese for garnish

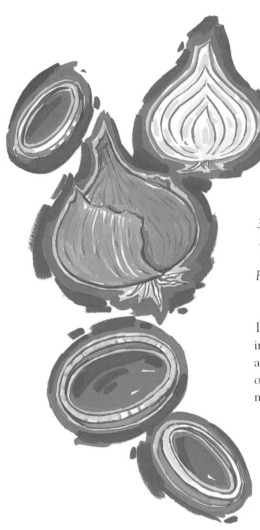

In a pot large enough to contain all the
ingredients, sauté the onions in the butter
and oil until they are just golden. Sprinkle
onions with flour and cook another 5
minutes or so, allowing the mixture to
 darken only slightly.

Stir in the hot broth, taking care to
keep the soup free of lumps. Season
with white pepper, drop in the
bouquet garni (remove before
serving), Gosling's Black Seal
Rum and simmer for 30 minutes.
Add a few generous dashes of sherry
peppers sauce just before serving.

Top each bowl with a round of French
bread sprinkled liberally with Gruyère
cheese and melted under the broiler.

Portuguese Red Bean Soup

2 large onions, thinly sliced
2 tbs good olive oil
1 lb chouriço sausage, skinned, chopped
4 potatoes, peeled and diced
2 cups dry red wine (Rioja is great)
4 cups low-salt chicken broth
two 19-oz cans of red kidney beans
1 lb fresh kale, trimmed, rinsed well, chopped fine (2 pkgs frozen)
1 bay leaf
generous pinch of cayenne pepper
2 tsp sugar

In a heavy-bottomed pot large enough to hold all the ingredients, sauté the onions and chouriço in the olive oil until the onions are softened and glazed. Pour off most of the fat. Stir in the potatoes and sweat them for a few minutes with the lid on. Add the wine and scrape up any clinging bits on the bottom of the pot. Add the chicken broth, beans, kale, bay leaf, cayenne and sugar.

Bring to a boil and simmer 1½ hours or longer, until the vegetables are tender. Skim fat occasionally. Remove bay leaf before serving hot with some crusty bread and sweet butter.

Island Black Bean Soup

FOR 6–8

The black, or turtle bean, has a distinctive flavour and is popular in tropical cooking. The soup should be a rich mahogany brown when completed.

1 lb dried black beans, soaked overnight
¼ cup (½ stick) butter
3 tbs olive oil
1 large onion, chopped
2 garlic cloves, chopped
4 cups good chicken broth
4 cups water
3 ribs celery, thinly sliced
1 tsp fresh thyme leaves
1 tbs parsley, minced
1 bay leaf
1 tsp allspice
½ tsp turmeric
2 tsp (or to taste) cumin
½ tsp cayenne pepper
½ tsp salt and freshly ground pepper to taste
¼ cup Gosling's Black Seal Rum
4 tbs sherry peppers sauce or to taste
chopped, hard-boiled egg, chopped onion and slices of banana for garnish

In a pot large enough to hold all the ingredients, sauté the onions and garlic in the olive oil and butter until golden. Add the beans, celery, thyme, parsley, bay leaf, and stir a few times to

26

warm them all up. Pour on the water and broth and bring to a boil. Simmer 3 hours until tender. Add the allspice, turmeric, cumin, cayenne, salt and black pepper and cook another 5 minutes. Now add the Gosling's Black Seal Rum and sherry peppers sauce and cook another few minutes. Remove from heat and purée somewhat less than half the beans. Return them to the pot, adding more broth if it becomes too thick. Garnish with chopped hard-boiled egg, chopped onion and a couple of banana slices.

Bermuda Pumpkin & Stilton Soup

Bermuda-grown pumpkins are green and white mottled outside, and bright orange within. For an easy sidedish—just steam, or microwave, mash and season with salt, pepper, allspice and lots of butter.

3 lbs Bermuda pumpkin, peeled, cubed
4 strips smoky bacon (or a link of chouriço sausage), chopped
1 large onion, chopped
3 cloves garlic, chopped
$^1/_2$ tsp dried sage
$^1/_2$ tsp thyme ground
$^1/_2$ tsp allspice
1 tsp salt
3 cups good chicken broth
$^1/_2$ cups light cream
3 tbs Gosling's Black Seal Rum
salt and freshly ground white pepper to taste
4 or so dashes sherry peppers sauce
$^1/_2$ cup Stilton cheese, crumbed for garnish

In a pot large enough to hold all the ingredients, sauté the bacon (or chouriço) until crispy. Remove, drain on a paper towel, crumble and reserve for garnish. Now sauté the onion and garlic in the bacon fat until translucent and well glazed. Drain off excess fat. Add the pumpkin and sweat, covered over

FISH STOCK

1 lb fish bones
1 tsp butter
$^1/_4$ cup fennel
2 small onions, chopped
1 leek, chopped, washed
2 ribs celery with leaves, chopped
1 clove garlic, crushed
2 cups white wine
2 cups water
bunch of parsley
8–10 peppercorns
1 whole clove
5 juniper berries
salt

Wash and chop fish bones and sauté them in the butter in a large pot, along with all the vegetables. Add the white wine and water and bring to a boil. Add parsley and spices and simmer for an hour. Strain through a fine sieve.

27

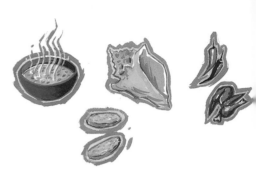

medium heat, for 5 minutes. Add the sage, thyme, allspice, salt and pepper and stir well.

Add the chicken broth and bring to a boil. Simmer for a half-hour or until the pumpkin is soft. Purée the soup in a food processor or blender, until smooth. Return to the pot, add Gosling's Black Seal Rum and most of the cream and re-heat, but don't boil. If it's too thick, thin with more cream or milk. Adjust seasonings with salt and white pepper, then add the sherry peppers sauce. Serve in warmed bowls, garnished with crumbled bacon (or chouriço) and Stilton cheese. Rich and satisfying.

Conch Chowder

Once upon a time, milk and harbour conch proliferated in Hamilton Harbour. That was before regular cruise ship arrivals. Today, conch are among many protected species in Bermuda.

1 lb queen conch (thawed), tenderised by smacking with meat mallet, chopped
3 cups clam broth
2 cups water
1 cup dry white wine
1 large onion, chopped
4 tomatoes, blanched, peeled, seeded and chopped
4 ribs celery, chopped
2 carrots, chopped

1 sweet red pepper, seeded, chopped
1 green pepper, seeded, chopped
1 large potatoe, random dice
2 tbs parsley, chopped
2 tsp fresh thyme
1 cup heavy cream
salt and white pepper to taste
3 tbs Gosling's Black Seal Rum
sherry peppers sauce

In a heavy-bottomed pot large enough to hold all the ingredients, simmer the conch in the clam juice and water for an hour. Add the wine, onions, tomatoes, celery, carrots, potatoes, parsley and peppers and simmer another hour. Add thyme, heavy cream, Gosling's Black Seal Rum, salt and white pepper to taste. Before serving, add a few dashes of sherry peppers sauce.

Khyber Pass Mulligatawny Soup

4 oz unsalted butter
4 medium onions
4–6 cloves garlic, minced

1 lb lentils, soaked overnight
1 tbs curry powder
2–3 dried hot chile peppers
2 red sweet bell peppers, chopped
2 tbs tomato purée
1 lb tomatoes, blanched, seeded, chopped
6 cups good chicken broth
4–6 cloves
2 tbs brown sugar
4 oz seedless raisins
salt and black pepper to taste
sherry peppers sauce to taste
toasted almonds for garnish

In a pot large enough to hold all the ingredients, sauté the onion and garlic in the butter until softened. Drain the lentils and add to the pot. Add the curry powder and peppers (hot and sweet) and stir. Add the remaining ingredients, mix well, bring to a boil and simmer 1½ hours. Remove the peppers, purée the soup to desired consistency. Adjust seasonings, adding the sherry peppers sauce just before removing from the heat. Sprinkle with toasted almonds.

Pineapple Curry Soup (cold)

Since the Age of Elegance, the pineapple has symbolised wealth and luxury. In Bermuda, its presence has always meant 'welcome.' The only fruit-bearing bromeliad, pineapple was introduced to Bermuda in 1616. So well did it adapt that Governor Wood wrote in 1633: "I wish I could send 1,000 pines in their season to the Queen…for I can well spare them."

2 large Bermuda, or other sweet onions, chopped
4 tbs olive oil
3 tsp good curry powder

CONCH

The milk—or harbour—and queen conch were once found in abundance in Bermuda's waters. The queen conch lays up to five-million eggs that hatch in about a week. They spend about three weeks as vulnerable plankton, finally settling to the bottom and looking more like tiny snails than anything else. The harbour conch prefers inshore waters; the queen, turtle grass near the outer reefs. Since 1978, both have been protected. The harbour conch, perhaps because of its less-violent habitat, has made a strong comeback; the queen has not. The conch shell was once used by fishermen to trumpet fish for sale. In Bermuda's whaling days, blowing the conch announced an incoming boat towing a whale.

*1½ lbs fresh pineapple, peeled, cored and
cut in chunks
3 tsp mild mango chutney
4 cups good chicken broth
juice of a lemon
1 cup of fresh or tinned pineapple juice
2 medium courgettes (zucchini), peeled,
chopped fine
2 tbs Gosling's Black Seal Rum
salt and white pepper to taste
½ pint whipping cream, whipped firm
¼ cup toasted almonds for garnish*

In a pot large enough to hold all the
ingredients, sauté the onions in the
olive oil until wilted. Add the curry
powder and stir. Add the chopped
pineapple and sweat for a minute or
two, stirring constantly. Add the broth
and bring to a boil. Add the pineapple
and lemon juice and stir. Add the
courgettes and simmer until all is
tender and soft. Stir in the chutney,
Gosling's Black Seal Rum, and remove
from the heat.

Blend to desired smoothness in a
food processor or blender. Adjust
seasonings and cool completely.
Remember, once chilled, the flavours
will be less pronounced. Serve cold,
garnished with a dollop of whipped
cream and a sprinkle of toasted
almonds.

SOUPS
AND
STARTERS

Carrot & Orange Soup

With a year-round carrot embargo,
Bermuda-grown carrots are the only
fresh ones available on the Island. Leeks
enjoy the same soil-enriching goodness
and season, as does the famous Bermuda
onion. A happy marriage of flavours.

*4 oz butter
1 large Bermuda, or other sweet onion,
chopped
2 large leeks halved, sliced and well-washed
2 cloves garlic, minced
1 tsp of curry powder
1 tsp ground ginger
2 tbs brown sugar
juice of 2 large oranges and the zest of 1
4 cups good chicken broth
1 lb carrots, peeled and chopped
¼ cup heavy cream*

In a pot large enough to hold all the
ingredients, sauté the onion, leeks and
garlic in butter until just wilted. Add
the curry, ginger and sugar, and stir for
a minute. Add the juice, zest and broth
and bring to a boil. Add the carrots
and simmer until softened. Purée in a
food processor or blender to desired
smoothness. Thin, if necessary, with a
little heavy cream. Serve cold (or hot)
garnished with a thin slice of orange.

Sunset Gazpacho

4 ribs of celery, minced (reserve the tops)
4 carrots, chopped fine
3 shallots, chopped
4 cloves garlic, chopped
3 cucumbers, peeled, seeded and chopped
3 bell peppers (green, red and yellow),
cored and diced
1 large onion, chopped
4 large tomatoes, blanched, seeded, chopped
1 tbs chopped fennel fronds
1/4 cup red wine vinegar
1 tbs Worcestershire sauce
3 tbs sherry peppers sauce or more to taste
2 tbs Gosling's Black Seal Rum
one 46-oz can tomato juice
1 bunch scallions, chopped fine
salt and pepper to taste
8 oz sour cream & minced parsley for garnish
1 cup prepared croutons

Put all the vegetables, except scallions, in a
food processor and pulse until you reach
the smoothness or chunkiness you desire.
Add the wine, Worcestershire sauce,
sherry peppers, Gosling's Black Seal Rum
and enough tomato juice to make a soup of
it all. Stir in the scallions, reserving some
for garnish and chill, preferably overnight
to allow the flavours to develop. Serve in
chilled bowls with a sprinkle of scallions,
parsley, a dollop of sour cream and croutons.

Appetisers

Three-Onion Pie

(Not as difficult as it looks)

4 tbs sweet butter
2–3 Bermuda leeks, chopped and washed
well
2–3 Bermuda onions, peeled and thinly-
sliced
1 red onion, peeled and thinly-sliced
1 tbs parsely, minced

2 egg yolks
1 cup light cream
1 cup heavy cream
freshly grated nutmeg
salt and white pepper
1/2 cup grated Gruyère or imported Swiss
cheese
one 9-inch pie shell of pâté brisée or bought
shell "blind-baked" (Page 32).

Sauté the leeks and onions in the butter
over a very low heat for 20–30 minutes
until softened and lightly coloured. Add
parsely and allow to cool while you
continue.

Whisk together the egg yolks and 2
creams in a bowl. Season with nutmeg,
salt and pepper to taste.

Spread the cooled onion-leek mixture
evenly around the bottom of the pie
shell. Sprinkle the cheese evenly over the

SOUPS
AND
STARTERS

31

PÂTÉ BRISÉE CRUST

This all-purpose dough may be refrigerated for a week or frozen for six months. Think of it as Play-Doh; it shapes and patches very easily. You may incorporate some fresh herbs into the dough for even more flavour.

2 cups flour
$\frac{1}{4}$ tsp salt
$1\frac{1}{2}$ sticks butter (cold), cut in pieces
2 tbs shortening (cold)
3 tbs iced water

Mix together the flour and salt. With a fork or pastry knife, cut the butter and shortening into the flour until it resembles a coarse meal. Add the iced water and work until a ball is formed. Knead the dough with the heel of your hand to evenly distribute the fat. Reform into a ball, wrap and chill until ready to use.

Roll the dough out to quarter-inch thickness and fit to your tart or pie pan. Chill again before use.

• *Blind baking means to pre-bake a pie or tart, shell empty. To prevent the shell from puffing up, a layer of waxed paper is put in the shell and weighted down with rice, dried beans or baking weights (pellets)—which are meant to be cooled, saved and re-used.*

SOUPS
AND
STARTERS

onions. Pour in the cream-egg mixture up to within a half-inch of the top.

Set the pie in the middle of a pre-heated oven (325 degrees) and bake for 45 minutes or until the top is somewhat browned on the edges and the custard firmly set.

Cool for at least 10 minutes before cutting into wedges. Serve warm.

Conch Fritters

$1\frac{1}{2}$ cups flour
2 tsp baking powder
$\frac{1}{2}$ tsp salt
$\frac{1}{4}$ tsp freshly ground pepper
$\frac{1}{2}$ tsp ground ginger
pinch of nutmeg
1 egg
$\frac{3}{4}$ cup milk
1 lb conch, finely chopped or ground
2 tbs onion minced
1 small clove garlic, minced
$\frac{1}{2}$ tsp thyme
1–2 jalapeño or habañero peppers, seeded, minced
lemon and lime wedges
vegetable oil for deep-frying

Combine the flour, baking powder, salt, pepper, ginger and nutmeg in a mixing bowl. Beat the egg together with the milk and stir quickly into the flour mixture. Do not overwork the batter.

Add the conch, onion, garlic, peppers

SHERRY PEPPERS, A HOT TOPIC

To the uninitiated, sherry peppers are both mystery and magic. The mystery is in the oft-asked question: what is a sherry pepper? And the magic is what it does to so many dishes. Well, sherry peppers are not peppers that taste like sherry, but rather an incendiary condiment beloved by locals and visitors alike.

It was during the 19th century that imaginative British Royal Navy sailors began fortifying casks of sherry with fiery hot peppers. They were concocting an all-purpose seasoning, a 'sauce,' if you will, intended to mask the often less-than-appetising flavour of ships' rations.

Stationed on Bermuda, at what was then one of the largest and most strategic naval dockyards in the western hemisphere, the sailors shared their favourite flavour with locals, who took it up with feverish fervour. Some old Bermudians favour vinegar peppers, perhaps the natural outcome of the wine's souring. Nearly every sideboard in Bermuda is graced by a cruet of sherry peppers sauce.

It is *the* Bermuda hot sauce, pre-dating the hot sauce craze by nearly a century. Commercial production by Yeaton Outerbridge began in 1964 as a cottage industry. Outerbridge's Original Sherry Peppers now produces more than 20 hot and spicy sauces, condiments and zesty soups.

Make your own simplified version by macerating a dozen or more of the hottest peppers you can find in a pint bottle of dry sherry. For wine vinegar peppers, substitute vinegar for the sherry. For rum peppers, submerge the peppers in Gosling's Black Seal Rum.

and thyme, stirring gently. Drop tablespoons of the lumpy batter into hot oil in batches—do not overcrowd. Fry until golden-brown (2 or 3 minutes).

Drain on paper towels and serve with lemon and lime wedges and a little mustard mayonnaise (mix Dijon mustard, mayonnaise and your favourite hot sauce to taste).

Shelly Bay Escargots

FOR 4

Shelly Bay is a calm beach on the North Shore, named for Henry Shelly, a member of the original Bermuda Company. It is ideal for children and non-swimmers.

1½ cups unsalted butter, softened
2 cloves garlic, minced
2 shallots, minced

2 tbs parsley, minced
a dash of Gosling's Black Seal Rum and
sherry peppers sauce
dash of Worcestershire sauce
generous pinch of curry
salt and freshly ground pepper to taste
1 tin 20-count snails (use French snails
only)
1 cup dry white wine
1 cup chicken stock
bouquet garni (parsley, thyme, bay leaf,
tarragon, chives, tied in a bundle)
1 garlic clove, chopped
2 small shallots, sliced
breadcrumbs for topping

Make the garlic butter by combining
the first 8 ingredients. Chill in the
fridge (or freeze for future use). Simmer
the snails for 5 minutes in a broth
composed of the wine, chicken stock,
bouquet garni, garlic, and shallots.

Drain and cool the snails, and place
in gratin or snail dishes. Mould a
healthy teaspoon of butter around each
snail. Sprinkle with breadcrumbs. Bake
for 15 minutes at 400 degrees. Don't let
the butter brown and turn bitter. Serve
immediately with crusty bread to soak
up the delicious, indulgent butter.

Chouriço in Flaky Pastry

Portuguese-Bermudians, most of
Açorean ancestry, make a fine, hot and
garlicky chouriço sausage—which they
pronounce "shah-deesh." Delicious
grilled on its own, or in soups and
other savoury dishes.

1 lb chouriço sausage, casing removed
two 1-lb packages of frozen puff pastry
sheets
2 egg yolks, beaten

Roll out the puff pastry fairly thin,
about $1/8$ of an inch. On a strip twice
the width of the sausage, place the
skinned sausage. Turn up the end of the
dough and roll the dough around the
sausage so it's totally 'wrapped.' Seal the
edges by brushing them with the beaten
egg and pressing together to form a tight
seal.

Now place the encased sausage on a
ungreased cookie sheet, seam side
down and brush with egg yolk to give
the dough a shiny 'finished' look. Bake
at 400 degrees until golden.

Slice and serve. Use a serrated knife
and be careful, for the dough will be
quite flaky. You may also make these
individually by slicing the sausage into
half-inch rounds and, with a cookie-
cutter, cutting out matching rounds a

quarter of an inch larger than the circle of sausage from the rolled-out dough. Then you simply sandwich the sausage between 2 circles of dough (brush the edges with egg to seal) and press together. Brush the tops with egg before baking and proceed as above. May be prepared ahead and frozen before baking.

Blind Dates

24 large pitted dates
3 small, sweet oranges, peeled and sectioned
1 tbs grated orange rind
1/2 cup Gosling's Black Seal Rum
8 slices bacon, cut in thirds
lemon crowns and parsley tufts for garnish

Combine the grated rind, Gosling's Black Seal Rum, orange segments and dates in a glass bowl. Allow to macerate for 4 hours or more. Stir once. Drain and reserve marinade (for use again). Wrap bacon around a date and orange segment and secure with a toothpick. Continue until all are assembled and lay out on a baking sheet. Broil about 4 inches from the heat until the bacon is crispy on both sides. Drain on paper towels and serve immediately. Garnish the tray with lemon crowns and parsley (they need colour).

Tropical Fruit Brochette

20 long sandwich picks, or short bamboo skewers, soaked in warm water
1 cup fresh orange juice
6 tbs guava paste (available in specialty markets)
1/4 cup Dijon mustard
1 tsp curry powder
1/4 tsp ginger, ground
2 tsp fresh lime juice
2 tbs Gosling's Black Seal Rum
about 80 chunks (total) of mango, papaya, loquat, pineapple, star fruit, kiwi, melon balls, etc.

Combine the juice, guava paste, mustard, curry, ginger and process in a blender until smooth. Put the mixture in a saucepan and simmer for 20 minutes. Remove from flame and add lime juice. Thread the fruit, alternating by colour or choice on the sandwich picks. Put them in a shallow glass or non-reactive pan, and pour on the marinade. Refrigerate overnight, turning a couple of times.

   Line a cookie sheet with foil and lay the brochettes in rows about 2 inches apart. Save marinade. Run under a pre-heated broiler for 2 minutes on each side. Serve warm with reserved marinade.

SOUPS
AND
STARTERS

35

Fish

MAIN
COURSES

Pan-Barbecued Wahoo

FOR 4

This popular local game fish is called the "speed merchant of the ocean." It is lean and tasty. Care should be taken not to overcook it.

four 8-oz wahoo steaks or 6-oz fillets
salt and freshly ground pepper to taste
2 tbs olive oil
³/4 cup Rum, Fire & Brimstone Barbecue Sauce (see Page 87)

Sauté the seasoned wahoo in olive oil until just golden on the edges (2 minutes a side). Drain excess oil. Add the barbecue sauce and cover. Simmer 8–10 minutes or until just cooked in the centre.

Wahoo with Bananas & Rum

FOR 6

6 wahoo fillets (about 6 oz each)
1 tsp salt
¹/2 tsp pepper
4 tbs flour
4 tbs unsalted butter (¹/2 stick)
¹/4 cup Gosling's Black Seal Rum
3 large or 6 small bananas, sliced lengthwise
2 tbs parsley, minced, halved orange slices for garnish

Mix the salt and pepper with flour, dredge the fillets in the mixture and shake off the excess. Melt the butter in a sauté pan and, just as it starts to foam, cook the fish on both sides until just cooked. Take care, this game fish overcooks easily. Remove from pan and

FINNY DELIGHTS More than 650 species of fish inhabit the waters around Bermuda. Yellowfin and blackfin tuna, amberjack, dolphin (mahi-mahi), pompano, gray snapper, red hind, coney, grouper, flying fish, hogfish and wahoo are among the edible catch brought in regularly. Game fish include: white and blue marlin, broadbill swordfish, sailfish, and mako shark. Spotted eagle rays are a common sight near the bridge at Flatts Inlet. The crystal-clear waters make the beauty of parrotfish and angelfish, cow polly and cute sergeant majors regular delights for snorkellers. Curiosities like moray eels, trumpet fish, seahorses, barracuda, octopus and squid are a regular part of the undersea fauna. See them at Bermuda Aquarium, Museum & Zoo.

keep warm. Add the remaining butter, the bananas and sauté for 2 minutes. Add the Gosling's Black Seal Rum and ignite. Flambé for 2 minutes, or until the flames die down. Pour over the fish. Garnish with bananas, a sprinkle of minced parsley and halved orange slices.

Stuffed Hogfish

FOR 4

So named for its hog-like snout, this reef- and harbour-dweller feeds almost entirely on shellfish and is particularly sweet-fleshed.

1 large whole hogfish (or sea bass)
1 tbs olive oil
2 scallions, white part only, sliced
1 clove garlic, minced
1/4 lb fresh mushrooms
2 tbs parsley, minced
1 tsp fresh thyme leaves
generous pinch of nutmeg
1 1/2 cup (more or less) fresh breadcrumbs
1/2 tsp sea salt
1/2 tsp freshly ground pepper
1 egg, beaten

Sauté the scallions, garlic and mushrooms briefly (2–3 minutes) in the oil. Remove from the heat. Toss in the parsley, thyme, nutmeg, breadcrumbs, salt and pepper and mix. Bind with the egg.

Wash the cavity of the fish and pat dry. Fill with the stuffing, packing it tightly. Close the opening with toothpicks. Place on an oiled roasting pan. Make 2 or 3 shallow little slashes along the body on both sides. Bake in a pre-heated, 450-degree oven for 20 minutes until the fish is firm and ready to separate from the bone. To serve, spoon out the stuffing onto the serving platter and lift portions from the frame along the slash lines. Some colourful steamed vegetables and plain, buttered rice go nicely.

St. David's Island Shark Hash

Although several species of shark occur on Bermuda's outer banks, the cub or dusky shark is the most common, but sand shark is best. It reaches a maximum length of about 12 feet, enough for plenty of hash. This dish should be spicy hot. You might want to open the windows when you cook the liver.

one 5-1b white, unspoiled shark, cut in large pieces, well washed
1 shark's liver, soaked overnight in vinegar or lemon juice and salt (should be white with no spots)
1 tbs olive oil
2 medium onions, minced
3 (or to taste) jalapeño (habañero,

serrano) peppers, seeded, minced
1 bunch parsley, minced
3–4 sprigs fresh thyme
salt
freshly ground pepper to taste

In a heavy-bottomed pot, put shark pieces and enough water to cover. Bring to a boil, lower to simmer and cook 1½ hours until the meat begins to shred. Remove from heat, strain and cool. With your fingers, remove the skin and bones. Put the shark in a double thickness of cheesecloth and wring out remaining moisture.

Sauté the liver in the olive oil to extract the oil from the liver and strain. Now sauté the onions and peppers in the oil until softened. Add the shredded shark, thyme and parsley and cook until flavours are well blended and the mélange is somewhat dried. For the dainty, serve warm spread on toast points, or by itself and have a bottle of hot sauce close at hand.

Conch Stew

1 medium onion, chopped
1 clove garlic, finely chopped
1 oz butter
1 lb conch meat, cleaned, diced
one 6-inch length of chouriço (or other hot) sausage, chopped (optional)
6½ cups fish stock (see Page 27)
2 medium potatoes, diced
2 ribs celery, sliced
2 carrots, diced

MAIN
COURSES

ST DAVID'S ISLAND There was a time when the only way to get to St. David's was by punt. The Islanders liked it that way. "I'm not Bermudjin, I'm a Sin' David's Islander," they'll tell you in a most friendly fashion. Old-timers still talk about Bermuda as being "over there," accompanied by a jerk of the thumb. They have their own ways, customs, traditions and patois, liberally sprinkled with archaisms.

In days past, most of the men went to sea as fishermen, as crew on merchant ships, worked as shipbuilders or were self-taught pilots who would scramble out to meet incoming freight or passenger ships and guide them safely to port. Farming also played a big part in the history of old St. David's. The finest arrowroot was once grown here, so was the Bermuda lily. Older residents remember Howard Farm on which Howard Smith developed the hardy, early-blooming *Lillium howardii*. Although no longer grown for export, full fields still burst into blossom every spring, here and there, throughout Bermuda. A lily bouquet is sent ever year, in time for Easter, to the Queen.

1 small turnip, diced
2 tomatoes, blanched, peeled, seeded, chopped
1 small green pepper, diced
1 tsp tomato paste
salt and pepper to taste
sherry peppers sauce or other hot sauce
1/2 tsp curry powder
fresh Bermuda thyme sprigs
1 tbs cornstarch
1 tbs parsley, minced

In a thick-bottomed saucepan large enough to hold all the ingredients, sauté the onion and garlic for a couple of minutes, then add the conch meat and sausage. Cook another 2 minutes. Add the fish stock, bring to a boil, lower heat and simmer for 1 hour. Now add all the vegetables, tomato paste, salt, pepper, curry powder and a few sprigs of thyme. Simmer for 1 hour. Dilute cornstarch in a little water and add to the hot stew to thicken. If a darker colour is desired, gravy browning may be used. Serve over plain boiled rice. Sprinkle with parsley and offer sherry peppers to tune it up.

Codfish Pie

This dish has been in the Lightbourn family since the time Bermuda traded salt from the Turks Islands for Nova Scotia codfish. Miss Phyllis Caisey, housekeeper and cook for the family for

three generations, shared her recipe with J.C. Lightbourn's son-in-law, Dick Butz, who shared his updated version with me.

1 recipe pastry dough (see Page 32)
1 1/2 lb salt cod, soaked overnight in water, changed once
1/2 lb bacon, chopped
1 large onion, shredded in strips
1 beef bouillon cube
1 1/2 cups water
1 1/2 tsp cornstarch
1 large potato, small dice
2 large carrots, small dice
1 large onion, chopped
1 tsp Tabasco or other hot sauce to taste
1 tsp Worcestershire sauce or to taste
salt and freshly ground pepper to taste

Rinse the cod and put in water to cover. Bring to a boil, then simmer for 10 minutes until cooked. Fry the bacon until translucent. Add the shredded onion and cook until softened.

Dissolve the bouillon cube in a cup of water and the cornstarch in the remaining water. Bring the beef broth to a boil, add the cornstarch and allow to thicken. Lower the heat slightly and add the potato, carrot and chopped onion. Season with Tabasco, Worcestershire, salt and pepper to taste. Add the cod and bacon to the mix and put filling in a large, glass, oven-proof bowl (or large porcelain soufflé dish). You

can make ahead to this point. Cover with pastry crust and bake for about 1 hour at 375 degrees, until golden.

FOR THE PASTRY
2 cups flour
2 tsp baking powder
1 tsp salt
1/3 cup olive oil
1/2 cup hot water
1 tsp fresh lemon juice
1 egg yolk, beaten

Mix together the flour, baking powder and salt. Make a well in the centre and put the oil, water, lemon juice and egg yolk. Mix together quickly to form a dough. Chill at least 2 hours in the fridge.

On a well-floured surface, roll out the pastry to 1/4-inch thickness and fit to baking bowl or dish. Use the trimmings to decorate the top with flowers or fish shapes to commemorate the event. If you are not adept at free-hand cutting, use small cookie-cutters—stars are nice. With a sharp- pointed knife make several 1/2-inch vent holes to allow steam to escape. Pastry may be made the day before; allow about a half-hour out of the fridge for dough to become pliable enough to roll out.

MAIN
COURSES

Sautéed Pompano
With Rum-Caramelised Shallots

FOR 4

1 lb shallots, thinly sliced
1 tbs peanut oil
1/4 tsp salt
2 cloves garlic, chopped fine
1 tsp fresh rosemary
freshly ground black pepper to taste
1/4 cup Gosling's Barbados Rum
1/2 cup fish broth or clam juice
juice of a lime
1 tbs heavy cream
1 1/2 lbs pompano fillets (or sole)
1 tbs unsalted butter
rosemary sprigs and lime slices for garnish

Sauté the shallots in the oil until softened. Add half the salt, garlic, rosemary and pepper and cook until the shallots are golden. Add rum, fish broth, lime juice and bring to a boil, stirring up any bits clinging to the pan. Reduce until the mixture becomes slushy. Add the heavy cream and cook another minute, stirring, and remove from flame. Keep warm.

Season the fillet with remaining salt and some pepper, and sauté in butter about 2 minutes on each side until opaque in the middle. Do not overcook. Lay a bed of caramelised shallots on each plate and lay a fillet on each. Serve with Pumpkin Fritters (Page 64).

The same is true with chips (French fries to you Yanks). Remove when golden-brown. Serve accompanied by crispy chips, and don't forget the malt vinegar.

Pub-Style Fish & Chips

FOR 4

1½ lbs white fish fillets (fresh cod, halibut, haddock, pollack)

FOR THE BEER BATTER
2 oz flour
salt and white pepper to taste
¼ cup beer or ale, more or less
vegetable oil for deep-frying

Season the flour with salt and pepper and whisk in the beer until the mixture is like a double cream and lump-free. Let rest for 15 to 20 minutes.

Be sure the oil is hot by dropping a small piece of bread or drizzling a bit of batter into the oil; it should immediately bubble up and crisp. Pat dry the fish fillets, dip and coat well with the batter and drop into the hot oil. Do not crowd them in—crowding defeats crispness.

Bermuda Escabeche

FOR 4

A popular West Indian dish. The word derives from the Spanish for pickled.

2 tbs olive oil
1 green bell pepper, seeded, sliced
1 red bell pepper
1 jalapeño pepper (or serrano, habañero), seeded, minced
2 onions, sliced thinly
1 tbs ginger root, minced
10–12 black peppercorns
⅛ tsp nutmeg
⅛ tsp allspice
1 bay leaf
salt to taste
⅔ cup water
3 tbs apple cider vinegar

1½ lbs yellowtail or flounder
¼ cup milk
¼ cup flour
salt and pepper to taste
¼ cup olive oil
2 tbs parsley, minced

Sauté the bell peppers, hot pepper, onions and ginger for 3 minutes in the

MAIN
COURSES

olive oil on a high flame. Add the peppercorns, nutmeg, allspice, bay leaf and salt and stir to warm. Add the water and bring to a boil. Simmer for 10–12 minutes, add the vinegar and cook a few minutes more. The sauce may be made ahead and re-heated.

Dip the fish fillets in milk, then in flour you have seasoned with salt and pepper. Sauté the fish in the olive oil until golden-brown, about 4–5 minutes, turning once. Transfer to plates, pour the hot sauce over the fish, sprinkle with parsley and serve. May be enjoyed warm, or at room temperature.

Grouper Amandine

FOR 6

Bermuda's most common commercial fish, the grouper can weigh up to 60 lbs.

6 pieces grouper fillet, about 6 oz each
1 tsp salt
1/2 tsp pepper
4 tbs flour

4 tbs unsalted butter (1/2 stick)
2 shallots, minced
1 tbs parsley, minced
1/4 cup sliced almonds, lightly toasted
parsley sprigs and lemon slices for garnish

Mix the salt and pepper with flour, dredge the fillets and shake off the excess. Melt the butter in a sauté pan and, just as it starts to foam, cook the fish on both sides until golden-brown on the edges. Remove from pan and keep warm. Add the remaining butter and the shallots, and sauté until softened. Add the wine and parsley and stir until slightly thickened. Add the almonds and pour over the fish. Garnish with parsley sprigs and lemon slices.

Dolphin Bermudiana

FOR 4

Of all game fish, the dolphin (the fish, not the mammal), or mahi-mahi, is rated best for eating. In Bermuda's waters, the average dolphin is 10–15

MAIN
COURSES

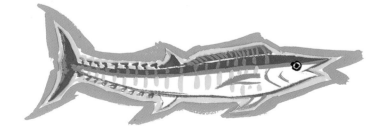

44

pounds. The sauce is part of the garnish for this pretty dish.

2 medium lemons
2 large oranges
6 tbs unsalted butter
1¾ lbs dolphin (mahi-mahi) fillets
cut in four ¾-inch-thick pieces
1 cup milk
1 cup all-purpose flour
2 tsp finely-chopped fresh mint
salt and freshly ground pepper
mint leaves for garnish

Using a sharp knife, peel the lemons and oranges, pare away the pith, and cut the fruit (remember to save the juices) in small dice.

In a large, heavy, non-aluminum casserole or skillet, melt 2 tablespoons of the butter over moderately high heat. Dip each fillet in the milk and then dredge in the flour, shaking off any excess. Add the fish to the pan and sauté until browned, 2–3 minutes each side. Remove to a platter and cover to keep warm.

In the same skillet, melt the remaining 4 tablespoons of butter. Add the diced fruit and reserved juice and cook until heated through, a half-minute or so. Stir in the chopped mint, season with salt and pepper to taste and spoon the sauce over the mahi-mahi. Serve immediately with plain, buttered rice, garnish with mint leaves.

CLAWLESS, OR THE BERMUDA LOBSTER

Lobsters are amazing creatures. They have thousands of eyes and are nearly blind; they hear with their legs, taste with their toes, have teeth in their stomachs and are—just look at them—second cousins to spiders. The spiny, clawless lobster (*Panulirus argus*), indigenous to Bermuda's waters, is one of 49 species caught in warm waters the world over.

It has been established that the Bermuda lobster is genetically identical to its Florida counterpart living more than 1,000 miles away. While some believe local lobsters reproduce and replenish their own numbers, others feel a significant percentage are expatriates that ride north on the Gulf Stream. Our clawless crustaceans, properly prepared, are every bit as tasty as 'true' lobsters, as taxonomists call the *Homarus americanus*, the clawed version found and fished only off the eastern coast of North America from North Carolina to Labrador. Bermudians have a deep affection for local lobster, and the season, running from September through the end of March, is eagerly anticipated.

45

Stuffed Spiny Lobster

four 1 1/2-lb lobsters, cooked and split, reserve the roe
1 cup of mushrooms, chopped
1/4 lb butter
1/2 cup flavoured breadcrumbs
2 tsp fresh thyme leaves
2 tbs dry vermouth
salt and pepper to taste
1/4 cup grated Parmesan or Pecorino Romano cheese, grated

Sauté the mushrooms briefly in the butter. Add the thyme and bread-crumbs and cook another couple of minutes. Add the roe, and finally a generous splash of vermouth. Adjust seasonings with salt and pepper. It should have an oatmeal-like consist-ency. Brush some oil or butter on the lobster shell to prevent burning. Stuff the lobsters with the mixture, sprinkle with cheese and run under the broiler for 2 minutes until just browned on top and all is hot and bubbly.

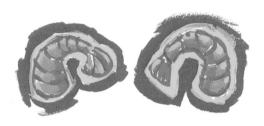

Sizzling Prawns with Rum

FOR 4

3 tbs peanut oil
1 Bermuda onion, chopped
1 small hot pepper (jalapeño, habañero, serrano), seeded, minced
2 tbs orange juice concentrate
zest of an orange
1/4 cup Gosling's Black Seal Rum

LOBSTER KNOWLEDGE

You may store a healthy live lobster for up to three days in the refrigera-tor. Don't put it on ice or in water; a little damp seaweed wouldn't hurt. Do not eat a lobster that has died. For every 1 1/2 lb of lobster, you get just more than 1/4 lb of lobster meat.

STEAMING A LOBSTER

Bring the water to a rapid boil and begin timing when the water returns to a boil.

1–1 1/4 lbs	12–15 minutes
1 1/2–2 lbs	15–20 minutes
2–3 lbs	20–25 minutes
3–6 lbs (you should be so lucky!)	25–28 minutes

$1^{1}/_{2}$ lbs large shrimp, peeled, tails on
salt and freshly ground pepper to taste

Preheat the oven to 500 degrees. Heat the oil in a large iron skillet and sauté the onions briefly. When the pan is sizzling, add the minced hot pepper, then the juice concentrate, zest and Gosling's Black Seal Rum. Bring back to heat and toss in the shrimp, turning to coat. Put skillet in oven and roast shrimp about 8 minutes, until pink. Serve sizzling.

Açorean Octopus Stew

FOR 6–8

4 lbs octopus, cleaned

FOR THE MARINADE
3 large cloves of garlic, minced
2 tbs paprika
3 tbs hot peppers, chopped
1 cup red wine

3 tbs Portuguese olive oil
3 large cloves garlic, minced
3 medium onions, diced
$^{1}/_{2}$ cup parsley, minced
salt and pepper to taste
1 tbs paprika
6 large potatoes, diced

Blanch the octopus in boiling water for 2–3 minutes to stiffen the tentacles and make them easier to cut. Drain, cool and cut into bite-sized pieces. Mix in a bowl with the marinade and refrigerate, covered, overnight.

In a large pot, sauté the garlic and onions in the olive oil until they're translucent. Add the parsley, salt and pepper to taste, paprika, octopus and the marinade and bring to a boil. Lower to a simmer and cook until the octopus is tender. Add the potatoes and cook until they are done and serve.

(Recipe thanks to Joseph Amaral)

Calamari with Bermuda Salsa

While squid is popular in many cultures, and the recipes diverse, the most popular is the simplest—deep-fried squid, or calamari fritti, to the Italians. Many Bermudians still feel the delectable mollusk is fit only for bait.

3 lbs squid (buy it already cleaned, cut into rings and tentacles)
about a cup of flour, well-seasoned with salt, pepper and cayenne pepper
3 or more cups peanut oil for deep-frying

Dry the rings and tentacles thoroughly with paper towels. Coat well with seasoned flour. I usually put the flour in a plastic bucket or paper bag and just

47

shake the squid gently until coated, and then, pardon the expression, fish them out. Heat the oil to 350 degrees, hot but not smoking. Test the heat by dropping a small piece in the oil—it should sizzle up immediately and come to the surface. Fry up the squid in batches, until golden. Do not crowd, as crowding defeats crispness. Drain well on paper towels. A fry basket, or Chinese mesh strainer makes retrieving cooked squid easy. Salt again if necessary. Serve with Bermuda Tomato Salsa (follows).

FOR THE BERMUDA SALSA
This has a nice smoky, hot and sweet character.

2 large ripe tomatoes
2–3 jalapeño peppers
1 Bermuda onion or other sweet onion
(Walla Walla, Vidalia), thick slices
2 cloves garlic, whole, on a skewer
½ tsp dried oregano
¼ tsp cumin
1 tbs Gosling's Black Seal Rum
¼ cup more or less water
½ tsp salt or to taste

Char the tomatoes, peppers, onions and garlic either over an open flame, on the grill or in a hot iron skillet until the skin blisters and turns black in spots—and in the case of the onion

MAIN
COURSES

and garlic, marks well and is softened. Rub off most of the charred tomato and pepper skin. Put all the ingredients in a food processor and pulse, adding water, until you reach a desirable, rough-textured salsa. Salt to taste. Use immediately or refrigerate up to 4 days. Serve at room temperature.

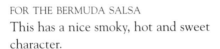

RUM FACTS
The Boston Rum Party?
Some say the American Revolution was not really about taxation and tea, but about rum. In an attempt to force the colonists to favour British over Spanish West Indian rums, the Molasses Act was passed in 1733. This placed a tax on molasses, sugar and rum imported from non-British West Indian islands. At the time, the rum consumption rate in the American colonies was three imperial gallons (3.75 American gallons) per year for every man, woman and child. This may have been, in fact, just the arrogant spark needed to ignite the revolution against King George.

Poultry

Roast Chicken Tropicale

FOR 6

one 5–6-lb chicken
salt and pepper
3 tbs olive oil
1 tsp cilantro, chopped
1 clove garlic, minced
$\frac{1}{4}$ cup pineapple juice (from tinned chunks)
juice of a lime
2 tbs Bermuda or other multi-floral honey
$\frac{1}{4}$ cup Gosling's Black Seal Rum
$\frac{1}{2}$ tsp fresh ginger, minced
3 tsp soy sauce
lime slices, hibiscus blossoms, and pineapple
chunks in syrup (reserved) for garnish

Rinse the cavity of the chicken with cold water and pat dry. Sprinkle inside with salt and pepper and truss legs closed.

Loosen the skin from the breast and legs by poking gently with your finger to separate. Mix half the olive oil with the cilantro and garlic and rub it in under the skin. Brush the chicken liberally with the remaining olive oil and salt and pepper the bird.

Mix together the reserved pineapple juice and syrup, lime juice, honey, Gosling's Black Seal Rum, ginger and soy sauce. Put chicken in a roasting pan and roast at 375 degrees, basting every 20 minutes with the rum pineapple glazing mixture for 1$\frac{1}{4}$ hours, or until the juices run clear from the thigh when pierced. Present whole surrounded by lime slices, hibiscus blossoms and pineapple chunks.

Portuguese Chicken

FOR 4

2 tbs Portuguese olive oil
2 tbs unsalted butter
2 large chicken breasts, split skin on (4 pieces in all)
1 medium onion, chopped
3 cloves of garlic, chopped
2 young sprigs of rosemary
$\frac{1}{2}$ cup dry white white
4 large ripe tomatoes, blanched, peeled, seeded, chopped
salt and freshly ground pepper to taste
2 tbs parsley, minced for garnish
sprigs of rosemary for garnish

Sauté the chicken breast in the olive oil and butter for 2–3 minutes a side until nearly cooked. Remove from the pan. Add the onions and garlic and sauté until just golden. Remove all but about a tablespoon of fat from the pan, add the rosemary and pour on the wine.

MAIN
COURSES

49

Raise the heat and cook until there remains 2 tablespoons or so of liquid, then add the tomatoes. Season with salt and pepper and simmer a few minutes.

Add the chicken and cover, poaching for about 5 minutes. Check to see the chicken is cooked to the bone. Serve generously sauced and sprinkled with chopped parsley and a sprig of rosemary as garnish.

Chicken Rosemary Barque

FOR 6

1 whole roasting chicken (5–6 lbs)
salt and freshly ground pepper to taste
3 large garlic cloves, halved
3–4 sprigs of fresh rosemary, leaves removed
3 sprigs parsley
2 lemons
3 tbs olive oil
1/2 cup good chicken broth
1/3 cup dry white wine
3 tbs unsalted butter
rosemary and parsley sprigs for garnish

Rinse the cavity of the chicken with cold water and pat dry. Sprinkle inside with salt and pepper and toss in the garlic, half the rosemary and the parsley sprigs.

With a carrot peeler, take the zest from one lemon and cut in julienne strips. Cut the peeled lemon in half and put in the cavity, and truss the legs closed. Loosen the skin from the breast and legs by poking gently with your finger to separate. Push the julienne of lemon and the remaining rosemary under the skin. Brush the chicken liberally with the olive oil, and salt and pepper the bird.

Put chicken in a roasting pan with the broth and roast at 375 degrees, basting occasionally for 1 1/4 hours or until the juices run clear from the thigh when pierced.

Place chicken on serving platter and keep warm. Remove as much surface fat from the pan juices as possible. Place roasting pan on stovetop and heat. Add the wine, squeeze in the juice of the remaining lemon and scrape up any clinging bits on the bottom of the pan. Boil and reduce liquid to about half a cup. Shut off heat, immediately whisk in butter and parsley, pour over bird and serve.

Orange Black Seal Rum Chicken

FOR 4

one 5-lb chicken, cut in eighths, skin on
one 6-oz can concentrated orange juice, defrosted
1/3 cup soy sauce

¼ cup Gosling's Black Seal Rum
1 small onion
4 cloves garlic, minced
1 tbs curry powder
½ tsp ground ginger
¼ tsp cayenne pepper

Mix together the above, put in a sealed plastic bag and allow chicken to marinate 4 hours or overnight in the refrigerator.

Place in a shallow roasting pan and roast in a pre-heated 375-degree oven for 45 minutes basting often with the marinade. Or, grill over the coals at a moderate heat, basting constantly until the skin is crisp and dark but not burnt. Serve with couscous or rice.

Bermuda Jerk Chicken

FOR 4

one 5-lb or so chicken, cut in eighths (or all thighs, all wings, as you like)

FOR THE MARINADE
2 tbs olive oil
¼ cup soy sauce
1 tsp gravy browning
½ cup apple cider vinegar
2 tbs ginger root, freshly grated
½ tsp nutmeg
½ tsp allspice
½ tsp cinnamon
4 Scotch bonnet (habañero) peppers,

seeded, roughly chopped
1 Bermuda onion, chopped
2 cloves garlic, chopped

Combine all the ingredients in a food processor and liquefy. Pour into a non-reactive pot and bring to a boil. Simmer 15–20 minutes until you reach desired thickness. Cool completely. Refrigerate in a clean, snap-lid jar. Keeps indefinitely. Can also be used on pork, beef or fish.

Wash the chicken, pat dry and put in a sealed plastic bag with the marinade for at least four hours, or better, overnight. Turn once or twice.

Place the chicken in a covered pan (a roasting pan with foil covering will do fine) with the marinade. Bake at 450 degrees for 20 minutes. Lower the heat to 275 and cook for another hour, basting occasionally. Remove from oven and serve as whole pieces or chopped into smaller pieces as they do 'down south' in the Caribbean. Pour some pan juices overall.

Alternatively, grill the chicken at least 6 inches from the hot coals. Slow-cook the chicken, basting frequently with the leftover marinade. Serve as whole pieces or chopped. Have a frosty pitcher of Dark 'n Stormy (Page 12) on hand to put out the fire.

MAIN
COURSES

51

Regimental Chicken Curry

6 boneless chicken breasts, cut in large dice
3 tbs butter
1 tbs peanut oil
1 onion, chopped
2 cloves garlic, chopped
1 tbs ginger root, minced
1 apple, diced
2 tbs hot curry powder
¼ cup flour
1 cup coconut milk*
1 cup chicken broth
salt and pepper to taste
Condiments served in little pots, traditionally called "boys"—chopped cucumber and yogurt, chopped peanuts, shredded coconut, loquat chutney, tomato chutney (both chutneys Page 89), raisins, chopped green onion, sliced banana.

MAIN
COURSES

Brown the chicken in the butter and oil in a heavy skillet and remove. Keep ready. If needed, add a little more butter to the pan and sauté the onions and garlic until golden. Add the ginger root, apples, curry powder and flour and stir well. Slowly stir in the coconut milk and chicken broth. Add the chicken and simmer for 20 minutes to allow the flavours to develop and the sauce to thicken. Adjust seasoning with salt and pepper. Serve with fragrant basmati rice, surrounded by "boys."

*Coconut milk is available tinned in Asian and speciality food stores. You may make your own by boiling together whole milk and grated unsweetened coconut, strain and cool before use.

Duck with Loquat Sauce

FOR 8

4 ducks
4 onions, halved
2 lemons, cut in quarters
4 large bay leaves
salt and freshly ground pepper
watercress for garnish

Rinse duck inside and out, pat dry. Salt and pepper the cavity. Insert a halved onion, 2 lemon quarters and a bay leaf into the cavity and truss it closed. In a pre-heated oven, roast the duck at 350 degrees for 1½ hours, pricking the skin once or twice during the cooking time to allow the fat to run out. The duck is done when the juices run clear from the thigh when pierced.

To serve: halve the duck, take the breast, back and thigh bone out. Arrange a half duck on each plate and reheat if necessary. Serve with loquat sauce and garnish with watercress.

FOR THE LOQUAT SAUCE
⅔ cup sugar

2 tbs cider vinegar
3 cups good poultry broth (use tinned broth
fortified by boiling with duck wings and
neck, parsley, celery, bay leaf and pepper-
corns for 20 minutes. Keep hot for use.)
1 cinnamon stick
3 tbs cornstarch diluted in 2 tbs cold water
1 tin loquats (Roland brand) with juice or
20 fresh, halved, peeled, seeded
¼ cup Bermuda Gold liqueur

Make a blond caramel by boiling the
sugar in 4 tablespoons of water until it
melts and goes golden. Quickly add the
vinegar, and the strained hot stock. Add
the cinnamon stick and simmer for 5
minutes. Add the juice from the can
(if using fresh, slightly decrease the
vinegar), Bermuda Gold liqueur and
bring to a boil. Thicken by adding the
cornstarch (more if necessary). If the
liquid is not boiling, the cornstarch will
not work its magic. Add the loquats,
remove the cinnamon stick, keep warm
or serve immediately. May be made
ahead and re-heated.

GET HOT!

To "get hot" in Bermuda
means to drink more than
is good for your ability to
reason. But getting hot,
to this cook, means using
fresh chile peppers (cap-
sicum) in a recipe. You
will see hot peppers
required in recipes
throughout this book. I
list them jalapeño, serrano,
habañero, in order of hot-
ness as they climb the
Scovil Ladder (not unlike
the Richter Scale for
earthquakes) towards
scorching. There are hun-
dreds of fresh and dried
chile peppers, from mild
and mildly hot to incendiary, and you should experiment to find your favourite. Smaller peppers are
usually hotter than big
ones. You can control
some of the fieryness by
removing the seeds and
inside ribs that store a lot
of the heat.

Peppers are among the
earliest cultivated plants,
dating back to 6200 B.C.,
and island cooking has
traditionally loved hot
peppers. Although
Bermuda has many
adopted West Indian
dishes, Bermudians don't
like their cuisine nearly as
hot as they do 'down
south.' Peppers add more
than heat to the pot.
Every chile has flavour
nuances, from citrus to
mango to smoky. The heat
comes from capsaicin. The
sensation triggers an
endorphin pain/pleasure
response that's part of the
appeal to hard-core pep-
per lovers.

The best antidote to a
real burner is not water or
beer that may intensify
the heat, but milk, ice-
cream, or bread, which
absorb and neutralise the
oils. Or just have a couple
of Dark 'n Stormies (Page
12). They won't dispel the
burn—you just won't care
anymore.

MAIN
COURSES

Meta

Curried Goat

5 lbs goat (or substitute lamb), cut in
1-inch cubes, fat trimmed
1 large onion, finely chopped
1 large green bell pepper, chopped
1 small chile pepper, seeded, minced (optional)
3 cloves garlic, crushed
2–3 sprigs fresh thyme, stripped of leaves
2–3 sprigs fresh parsley, minced
4 tbs good curry powder
1½ tbs seasoned salt
½ tsp accent
generous pinch black pepper
2 bay leaves
¼ cup more or less peanut oil
3–4 cups chicken broth
2 large carrots, diced
3 large potatoes, peeled, diced

MAIN
COURSES

Put everything except the oil, broth,
carrots and potatoes into a large bowl.
Rub down the goat meat with all the
spices and let it marinate for 1 hour.

Heat the peanut oil in a heavy-
bottomed pot large enough to hold all
the ingredients. When the oil is quite
hot, sauté the goat in batches, browning well. Remove the meat and set
aside. Lower the heat and add the
onions, peppers (from the marinade),
and sauté until the onions have wilted.

De-glaze the pot with some of the
broth and scrape up the clinging bits
on the bottom. Add the remaining
broth, the meat and bay leaves and
simmer for 2 hours. Add the potatoes
and carrots (more broth if necessary)
and simmer another hour, or until the
meat is very tender. Serve over warm,
buttered rice or with freshly-baked roti
(floppy, golden, griddle bread) or
Johnny cakes (Page 65).

(Adapted from a recipe by Sharon Stevens)

Pawpaw Montespan

FOR 4

The name comes from the Montespan
Lodge in Warwick Parish, where the
casserole, it is said, had its origins.

2 tsp butter
2 large onions, chopped
1 lb ground beef
4 green pawpaws, peeled, halved, seeded
6 ripe tomatoes, sliced
1 cup grated Parmesan cheese
plain breadcrumbs or cornflakes crumbs
salt and freshly ground pepper

Sauté the onions in butter until softened. Add the ground beef, season

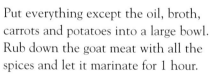

THE WEST INDIAN INFLUENCE

Slavery brought West Indians to Bermuda. The first mention of slaves in Bermuda records is in 1617. While some came to Bermuda on merchant ships from Africa, white slaves came from Scotland and Ireland, but most slaves came from the West Indies. Like any ethnic group, they brought with them their traditions and food. Bermuda's salt-trading days in the Turks & Caicos Islands, beginning in 1678, also helped bring new flavours to the table.

Like the vast majority of flora and fauna in Bermuda, many of the fruits, vegetables and delicacies were imported and naturalised long ago. The cassava root, a tuber,

was surely a West Indian import, as were the paw-paw and christophine. The yam-like West Indian dasheen were called "eddoes" here when they were cultivated. The cherimoya or custard apple was naturalised, as were the mango, guava, passion fruit, plantains, bananas, oranges, lemons, pomegranates, sugarcane and figs. Many of these fruits were under cultivation by the late 17th century, and were even exported to London and the colonies in Virginia, New York and New England.

The use of curry (*colombo* in the Caribbean) arrived here before the first East Indian immigrants. The everyday staple of beans and rice came from down south,

too. To be sure, the first hot peppers to go into the pot were put there by West Indians.

The Spanish word, *escabèche*, meaning pickled, and referring to fried fish pickled in vinegar, comes into the local food lexicon by way of the Spanish influence on West Indian cooking that began in the 15th century. Some Bermudians say "caveeched" fish.

Curried goat, curried mussel pies, jerk chicken and pork, conch stew, roti, fish with bananas and rum, peas and rice, are some of the direct descendants, products of a happy culinary inter-marriage which became part of Bermudian cuisine via the West Indian influence.

MAIN COURSES

with salt and pepper, and cook until it loses its colour. Drain and keep ready. Boil the pawpaws until tender. Drain, mash with a fork, salt and pepper to taste. In a buttered casserole, put down a layer of the pawpaws. Put a layer of

the ground meat mixture on top. Now layer on slices of tomato, dust with grated cheese, liberally sprinkle with the breadcrumbs and dot with butter. Bake at 350 degrees for 30 minutes or until bubbling hot and golden on top.

Steak 'n Kidney Pie

The filling may be made ahead and improves after a night in the fridge. Frozen puff pastry makes this an easy, tasty dish.

2 lbs top round beef cubes (for stewing)
1/2 lb (more or less) veal or lamb kidney cleaned* and sliced
2 large onions, chopped
1/2 lb small mushrooms or halved as necessary
2 tbs butter
1 tbs vegetable oil
3/4 cup of flour
1 tsp thyme
1 tsp marjoram
salt and freshly ground pepper to taste
2 tsp fresh parsley, chopped
1 cup decent red wine
1 cup low-salt beef stock
1 box frozen puff pastry sheets
1 egg, beaten

In a pot large enough to hold all of the ingredients, sauté in a little butter the onions and mushrooms until the onions are translucent. Remove with a slotted spoon and reserve. Add the remaining butter and the oil.

Combine the flour, thyme, marjoram, salt and pepper in a bowl and dredge in the meats. Turn up the heat and brown the meat cubes and kidney on all sides (in batches if necessary). Deglaze the pot by pouring in some of the wine and scraping up the clinging bits on the bottom. Add the onions and mushrooms, then the remaining wine. Bring to a boil and add the beef stock. Bring again to a boil, lower flame, add the parsley and simmer an hour or more until the beef is fork-flaking tender, the sauce rich and dark. You may cool and save (even freeze), or proceed.

Fill individual serving bowls with some of the 'stew.' Top with a piece of the defrosted puff pastry, cut slightly larger than the top of the dish. Use an over-turned dish as a template to cut along. Brush the fitted pastry with beaten egg just before popping into a 400-degree oven. Bake until the pastry is golden and crispy and the inside all bubbly and hot. A grilled tomato topped with herbed breadcrumbs is an appropriately "pubby" accompaniment.

* Cleaning kidneys can be tedious. Remove the gauzy membrane, then make an incision and carefully cut out all the little tubes inside. Rinse under cold water and proceed.

Shepherd's Pie

ABOUT 4 HEARTY SERVINGS

Originally this pie had a proper pastry crust. Somewhere during its evolution, that was replaced by a lid of mashed potatoes. The original also called for ground lamb, but today beef prevails. I use both, cubed, not ground.

½ cup flour
salt and freshly ground black pepper to taste
1 lb beef, cubed
1 lb lamb, cubed
¼ cup olive oil
2 onions, diced
2 garlic cloves, chopped
2 bay leaves
2 tsp of thyme
2 tbs fresh parsley, minced
approximately 1 cup of low-salt beef broth
6 or more potatoes, boiled, whipped with salt, pepper, 3 oz heavy cream, 2 eggs to bind
pinch of cinnamon

Season the flour with salt and pepper and dredge the meat cubes in the mix. Sauté the onions and garlic in olive oil until translucent. Add the cubed meats and brown well. Drain off excess fat. Add the herbs, cinnamon and cook another minute.

Pour on a little broth and scrape up the clinging bits on the bottom of the pot. Add remaining broth to cover and bring to a boil. Lower the flame and cook until the meat is beginning to shred, and the sauce somewhat thickened. Can be made ahead.

Fill individual serving dishes three-quarters to the top with the meat

mixture. Pile the whipped potatoes into a pastry bag fitted with a large decorative tip and pipe the potatoes on top, or trowel them on nicely. When ready, bake in a hot, 400-degree oven for 15–20 minutes, or until the potatoes have begun to brown here and there, and the meat mixture is bubbling hot.

Beef Short Ribs with Rum & Peaches

FOR 4–6

3 onions, chopped
2 tbs light olive oil
3 lbs beef short ribs
salt and freshly ground pepper to taste
1 cup water
1 cup beef broth
2 tsp ground ginger
one 28-oz can peach halves (save the juice)
2 tbs soy sauce
3 tbs cornstarch
¼ cup Gosling's Black Seal Rum
2 sweet bell peppers (one red, one green) cut in strips

Sauté the onions in the oil until softened and remove. Season the ribs with salt and pepper, and brown on all sides in the oil. Drain excess fat. Add the water, broth, ginger and cooked onions and bring to a boil. Simmer for 2 hours or until tender.

MAIN COURSES

In another heavy-bottomed pot, combine the peach juice, soy sauce and sweet peppers and bring to a boil. Moisten the cornstarch with the Gosling's Black Seal Rum and add to the boiling liquid. Stir until thickened. Lower the heat, add the peaches and cook until just heated through. Place the short ribs, onions and a little juice on a platter and ladle on the sauce and peach halves. Pretty—and very tasty.

Bermuda-Style Brisket of Beef

FOR 4–6

The author of this crockpot dish says he likes to "put it on in the morning and forget about it until we're ready to eat."

5–6 lb brisket of beef
2–3 pawpaws, peeled and sliced about ¼-inch thick
4 large potatoes
3 medium onions, sliced
4–6 carrots, peeled and sliced into 'coins'
2 cups water
2 tbs soy sauce
2 tbs Worcestershire sauce

Put the beef on the bottom and layer everything else on top in order of appearance. Add the water, soy and Worcestershire and let it cook all day. Serve with a nice salad of fresh greens and a simple vinaigrette dressing.

(Adapted from a recipe by nonagenarian Edward Churm, an enthusiastic home cook who "likes to see 'em happy when they eat.")

Pasta with Chouriço

FOR 4

1 lb penne (ziti, rigatoni, or your favourite shape)
2 large links hot chouriço sausage, cut in pieces
1 tbs olive oil
1 medium onion
2–3 cloves garlic
28-oz tin of Italian-style tomatoes, seeded, chopped (save the juices)
1 tsp fresh rosemary leaves
2 tsp fresh thyme leaves
6 fresh basil leaves
1 tbs parsley, minced
salt and freshly ground black pepper to taste
¼ cup grated Pecorino Romano or Parmesan cheese

Sauté the sausage pieces in the olive oil until browned on the edges. Remove with a slotted spoon. In the same pot, sauté the garlic and onions in the remaining oil until softened. Add herbs and heat them for a minute. Add the tomatoes, some reserved juices, and stir well. Simmer for 20 minutes, stirring occasionally. Return

MAIN
COURSES

the sausage pieces to the pot and cook another 5 minutes. Adjust seasonings.

Cook the pasta in plenty of well-salted boiling water until *al dente*, or just cooked. Drain and toss with the chouriço tomato sauce. Serve in warmed bowls.

Pork Tenderloin with Hot Pepper Sauce

FOR *4*

2–3 pork tenderloins (about 1½ lbs total)
2 tbs peanut oil
1 medium onion, chopped
2 cloves garlic, chopped
2 tsp cumin
½ tsp salt or to taste
4 dried ancho peppers, softened in hot water (25 minutes), chopped
1 tbs apple cider vinegar
¼ cup fresh orange juice
½ cup chicken broth
3 tbs dark brown sugar
¼ cup ketchup

2 tbs Gosling's Black Seal Rum
orange slices for garnish

Sprinkle the pork loin with salt and pepper and in an iron skillet, brown on all sides in half the oil. Transfer the skillet to a pre-heated 350-degree oven and cook for 15 minutes or until just done.

Meanwhile, make the sauce by sautéing the onion and garlic in the remaining peanut oil until softened. Add the cumin, peppers, vinegar, juice, broth and brown sugar and bring to a boil. Add the ketchup, salt and Gosling's Black Seal Rum and simmer until the peppers are very soft. Purée the mixture in a blender of food processor until smooth, adding chicken broth to desired thickness. Can be made ahead.

Slice the cooked tenderloin into medallions about ½-inch thick, nap each plate with a little sauce and lay the medallions on top. Garnish with orange slice. Equally tasty with grilled steak or chicken.

MAIN COURSES

WHOLE HOG

Bermuda knows how to dignify its first inhabitants. When settlers arrived in these Islands, among the only living creatures were skinks (an endemic, now rare lizard-like reptile); birds (Audubon shearwater, and the Bermuda petrel, called the cahow) and wild hogs. Surely it was a surprise to find pork in nature's larder. The hogs were believed to have been off-loaded by Spanish explorers. The tasty hogs were commemorated on Bermuda's first coin. Minted during the reign of King James I, so-called "Hogge money" was the earliest coinage minted for a British colony. The silver-plated, copper coins were in circulation from about 1616 to 1624 and prohibited from export. The contemporary Bermuda one-cent coin still sports the vanished wild hog.

Sides
Salads
&
Sandwiches

Sides

Hoppin' John

A big Bermuda favourite and a regular on picnic and get-together menus. Identical to Peas & Plenty, a New Year's Day dish in Bermuda, as in the American South. Eating whole beans, in which is secreted a shiny new coin, on January 1 helps ensure there will be prosperity in the coming year.

2 cups long grain rice
1 lb black-eye peas
2 tsp fresh thyme
½ lb smoky bacon
2 Bermuda onions, chopped
1 clove garlic, chopped
¾ lb chouriço sausage, chopped
salt and freshly ground black pepper to taste
Tabasco sauce to taste

Boil the peas and thyme until the peas have split. Drain, reserving about a quarter cup of water with the peas. In a deep, heavy-bottomed pot, fry up the bacon until just crisped and remove with a slotted spoon. In the same pot, add the onion, garlic and chouriço, cook until golden and the chouriço just browned. While this is going on, boil the rice in plenty of well-salted water until tender. Drain and keep ready.

Drain off most of the fat. Add the peas and water, stir and cover a few minutes. Add the cooked rice and reserved bacon and mix well. Cook over lowest heat until nearly dry. Take care not to scorch the mixture. Adjust seasoning with salt, pepper and Tabasco sauce.

Spanish Rice

4 slices of bacon, chopped
1 large onion, chopped
2 cloves garlic, chopped
½ cup white rice
1 large green or red bell pepper, chopped
one 19-oz can whole tomatoes, seeded, chopped (save juice)
2 cups chicken broth
½ tsp salt
grated Parmesan cheese (optional)

Sauté the bacon in a heavy-bottomed pot large enough to hold all the ingredients. As the bacon approaches the crispy stage, add the onions and garlic and sauté them until softened. Add the rice and bell pepper and cook, stirring about 3 minutes. Add the tomatoes, juice and chicken broth and bring to a boil. Add the salt and rice and cook until tender. If all the liquid has evaporated before the rice is fully cooked, add more broth or water until done. Some cooks sprinkle the rice with grated Parmesan before serving; some don't. I do.

Red Beans & Rice

FOR 8

1 lb dried small red beans, soaked overnight
1 ham bone and scraps, or 2 meaty ham hocks
1 lb chouriço sausage
4 tbs bacon drippings, or olive oil
3 large onions, chopped
2 cloves garlic, chopped
$1/2$ cup parsley, chopped
1 cup dry red wine
8 cups ham stock, or chicken broth
2 cups white rice, cooked
salt and ground pepper to taste
Louisiana-style hot sauce to taste

In a heavy-bottomed pot, sauté the ham bone and ham scraps,

or the ham hocks, and chouriço in bacon drippings for about 5 minutes. Add the onions and garlic and sauté them until softened. Add the parsley, beans, wine and enough stock to cover. Bring to a boil, reduce heat and simmer for 2 hours uncovered. Remove the ham bone, or hocks, and return any bits of meat to the pot. At the end of the cooking time, when the beans are tender, purée one cup of beans in a blender, or food processor, and return to the pot to thicken. Season with salt, freshly ground black pepper and hot sauce to taste. Serve over, or mixed with, cooked white rice.

Macaroni & Cheese

FOR 8–10

Very popular and a consistent menu item in small, home-style restaurants and, indeed, in many homes. Everybody has their version, of course. Here's mine.

2 lb elbow macaroni
$1^1/2$ lbs (or more) sharp Cheddar cheese (the good stuff) grated
$1/4$ lb butter
2 medium onions, minced
$1/2$ cup all-purpose flour
6 cups whole milk

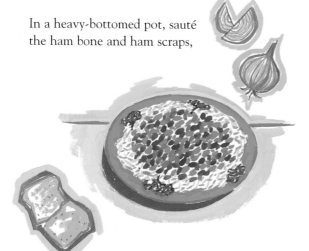

1 tbs fresh parsley, minced
1 tbs Dijon mustard
2 tbs mayonnaise
1 tbs paprika
2 tsp white pepper
³/₄ cup unflavoured breadcrumbs

Cook elbows in well-salted boiling water until *al dente* (do not over-cook). Drain and rinse in cold water. Sauté the onions in half the butter until translucent. Add flour and blend until smooth. Stir in milk, beating until smooth and cook about 5 minutes.

Blend grated Cheddar cheese, parsley, mustard, mayonnaise, white pepper and paprika into sauce and blend all together with macaroni. Spoon the fairly gloppy combination into a 4-quart casserole (a pretty one you'll want to serve in). Sprinkle all over with breadcrumbs, dot with remaining butter and bake at 350 degrees for 45 minutes or until bubbly and golden on top and browned at the corners (my favourite part).

Variations: add minced jalapeño pepper, or ³/₄ lb cooked, crumbled bacon, or 1 cup of julienned smoked ham, or a medium-sized can of well-drained tinned tuna or crab meat to the mixture.

Stuffed Christophines

FOR 4

Also called *mirliton* by the French, and *chayote* in the American Southwest, this pale-green avocado-shaped vegetable is fairly bland and resembles vegetable marrow in taste and texture. At weekend yard sales, I have found these garden-grown cuties displayed for sale among the housewares and antiques!

2 christophines, cut in half lengthwise
¹/₄ lb (one stick) unsalted butter
¹/₂ lb chouriço sausage, chopped
1 large onion, chopped
1 clove garlic, chopped
2 ribs celery, chopped
1 large bell pepper, chopped
3 scallions, white and green parts sliced
¹/₂ lb shrimp, shelled, deveined, chopped
¹/₂ tsp basil
1 tsp fresh thyme
¹/₂ tsp cayenne pepper or to taste
1 tsp Worcestershire sauce
about 1 cup seasoned breadcrumbs

Cover and boil the christophines in water until the flesh is tender (20–30 minutes). When ready, drain, cool and remove the seeds. Scoop out the pulp, leaving a ¹/₄-inch of pulp and chop. Save the shells.

Meanwhile, sauté the chouriço sausage in the butter until browned.

Add the onion and garlic and cook until softened. Add the celery, bell pepper and scallions and cook another couple of minutes. Toss in the shrimp and spices and cook only until they turn pink on both sides. Add the Worcestershire and cooked, chopped christophine, stir to combine and remove from the heat. Add enough breadcrumbs to bind the stuffing. Adjust seasonings. Re-fill the scooped-out shells with the stuffing and bake in a pre-heated 350-degree oven for 20–30 minutes. Take care not to dry them out.

Pumpkin Fritters

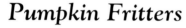

MAKES ABOUT 24, DEPENDING ON SIZE
1 cup flour
1/2 cup sugar
generous pinch of salt
1 rounded tsp nutmeg, freshly grated
1/2 tsp baking powder
1 cup water
one 1-lb tin pumpkin purée or 2 lbs fresh Bermuda pumpkin, cooked, mashed, drained
oil for frying (about 2 cups)

In a large bowl, combine the flour, sugar, salt, nutmeg and baking powder. Make a well in the centre and add the water, slowly drawing in the flour until blended. Mix in the pumpkin until well combined. Let stand 20–30 minutes at room temperature before proceeding.

Heat the oil in a deep-fryer or iron skillet, hot but not smoking. Drop batter by tablespoonsful into the oil, don't crowd or they won't brown nicely. Turn and cook on the other side—it should take no more than 5 minutes. Remove with Chinese strainer or slotted spoon. Drain on paper towels and serve while hot.

Cornbread

Since cornbread goes so well with chili, and chili is for a crowd—this will make enough for about 18 servings. The recipe may be scaled down, of course. Can be made in corn-shaped iron moulds, skillets—even as cute muffins.

4 cups unbleached flour
3 cups yellow cornmeal
1 cup sugar
4 tbs baking powder
1/2 tsp cayenne pepper (or 1 tsp of cracked black pepper)
2 tsp salt
8 eggs
4 cups whole milk

Grease two 13 x 9-inch glass or metal roasting pans. In a bowl, combine flour, cornmeal, sugar, baking powder, pepper and salt. In another bowl, beat the eggs and milk together. Add the cornmeal mixture to the milk and eggs, stirring just to combine. It will be lumpy—do not over-mix. Pour the batter into the baking pans, skillets or muffin tins. Bake in a preheated 350-degree oven for 30 minutes or until the tester comes out clean. Cool in the pan and cut into squares or wedges.

Variation: You can, if you like, add a cup of frozen corn kernels to the recipe, or a cup of grated Cheddar cheese—or both!

Rum-Honeyed Onions

FOR 4–6

1 lb small onions
¼ cup Bermuda honey or other multi-floral honey
2 tbs unsalted butter
¼ cup Gosling's Black Seal Rum

Boil onions in salted water until tender, but still firm. Drain and remove skins. In a large sauté pan, heat together the honey, butter and rum. Add the onions and cook until well glazed with the sauce, spooning the sauce over the top and rolling the tasty onions around until just softened. Serve hot.

Johnny Cake

It is generally agreed Native Americans taught the English settlers how to make cornmeal cakes. Some link it to the American Indian word *joniken*, while some called them "journey" cakes.

1 cup flour
1 cup cornmeal
½ cup sugar
½ tsp salt
1 tsp baking soda
¾ cup buttermilk

Sift together the dry ingredients. Add the buttermilk and form 6 small balls. On a floured surface, press them out to 1-inch thickness and 'bake' on a hot, oiled griddle or skillet, 3 minutes a side until slightly risen and golden.

RUM FACTS
Poetic Licence
Planter's Punch, dating from the 17th century, may be the oldest rum and fruit refresher. The rhyming recipe of yore is: "one of sour, two of sweet, three of strong and four of weak." That is, one of lime juice to two of sugar, three of rum and four of ice. A little later, other fruit juices were added, but you get the idea (see recipe on Page 15).

SIDES,
SALADS &
SANDWICHES

Salads

Sub-Tropical Fruit Salad

FOR 6

2 pink Bermuda grapefruit
2 large sweet oranges
1 ripe mango
2 ripe Bermuda avocado pears
1 ripe Bermuda pawpaw (papaya)
1/4 cup Bermuda honey or other multi-
floral honey
juice of a lime
zest of a lime
pinch of salt
1/4 cup Gosling's Rum Deluxe
1 large head bibb lettuce
6 Bermuda strawberries (world's best)
mint sprigs for garnish

Peel the grapefruits and oranges of all skin and pith. Cut in 1/2-inch-thick rings, then into quarters. Peel, pit and slice mango and avocado. Peel, seed and cube the pawpaw. Put all the fruit in a shallow bowl or glass roasting pan.

Beat together the honey, lime juice, lime zest, salt and rum. Drizzle the dressing over the fruit and refrigerate for one hour. Arrange a bed of lettuce on each plate, mound or decoratively arrange the fruits, plant a strawberry and mint sprig in an appropriate spot and serve.

Shrimp & Fruit Salad

FOR 4–6

1 lb medium shrimp, peeled, tails on
2 small limes, peeled, diced
1 pineapple cut chunks, save any juices
1/4 cup Gosling's Black Seal Rum
1 hot pepper (serrano, habañero), seeded, minced

4 nectarines ripe, stoned, cut in wedges
1 lemon, peeled, diced
2 kiwi, peeled, sliced
2 purple plums, ripe, stoned, cut in wedges
2 green plums, ripe, stoned, cut in wedges
1/2 pint blackberries
a sprig of fresh dill, chopped
a head of bibb lettuce

Marinate the shrimp with the lime, pineapple and juice, Gosling's Black Seal Rum and hot pepper for about 1 hour at room temperature. Meanwhile, make a nice salad out of the remaining fruit. Chill.

Skewer the shrimp and pineapple seperately. Grill the shrimp until just done and the pineapple chunks well warmed. Arrange the fruit salad on the lettuce and the shrimp and pineapple on top of all.

SIDES,
SALADS &
SANDWICHES

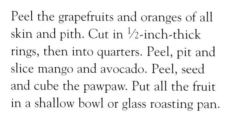

Tucker's Town Lobster Salad

FOR 2

Don't forget to ice some champagne.

cooked tail meat of two 1½-lb spiny lobsters
cut in medallions about ½-inch thick
1 egg yolk
⅓ cup olives
2 tbs fresh lemon juice
4 dashes of Tabasco
pinch of salt
¼ cup fresh dill, finely chopped
1 cup celery, thinly sliced
⅓ cup chopped pimento
¼ cup scallions, thinly sliced
1 large head Boston lettuce
lemon crowns and dill sprigs for garnish
salmon caviar for garnish

In a blender, or food processor, allow the yolk to spin until thickened (4–5 minutes). Slowly drizzle in the olive oil until a thick mayonnaise is formed. With the machine still whizzing, slowly add the lemon juice, Tabasco and salt. Scrape the mayonnaise into a bowl. Fold in the dill, celery, pimento and scallions and finally the lobster. Line glass plates with lettuce leaves and mound the lobster in the centre of each plate. Decorate each plate with a lemon crown, a dollop of salmon caviar and a plume of dill. Really, darling!

Showboat Salad

FOR 4

Minted chicken salad in pineapple boats.

3 tbs peanut oil
2 lbs boneless chicken, in bite-sized pieces
3 tbs ginger root, minced
2 cloves garlic, minced
¼ tsp red pepper flakes
¼ cup Gosling's Black Seal Rum
⅓ cup chicken broth
½ cup fresh mint, chopped
½ cup mayonnaise
½ cup yogurt
juice of a lemon
zest of a lemon
½ cup scallions, sliced
1 large banana, chunked
1 mango, peeled, pitted, chunked
1 ripe pawpaw (papaya), peeled, seeded, sliced
2 kiwi fruits, peeled sliced in thick rounds
2 pineapples, cut in half, fruit removed in chunks, save shells
salt and white pepper to taste
mint sprigs for garnish

Sauté the chicken in the oil along with half the ginger and half the garlic and red pepper. Remove from the pan when just cooked through. De-glaze the pan with the Gosling's Black Seal Rum, add the chicken broth and bring to a boil. Add half the mint. Boil down until only 2–3 tablespoons of liquid remains. Cool.

SIDES,
SALADS &
SANDWICHES

Make a dressing by blending together the mayonnaise and yogurt, lemon juice, zest, reduced minted broth, remaining garlic, mint and ginger. Adjust seasonings to taste. Toss the cooled chicken with the chilled dressing and add the fruits and scallions. Chill for a couple of hours to allow the flavours to develop. Fill the hollowed pineapple shells with the chicken and fruit mix. Garnish with mint sprigs and serve.

Tomato Onion Salad

Simple, irresistible.

4 perfectly ripe medium Bermuda
tomatoes, thickly sliced
1 large Bermuda onion (or other sweet
onion), thinly sliced
1 tbs fresh oregano leaves, chopped
8–10 fresh basil leaves, thinly sliced
pinch of salt
4–6 tbs balsamic vinegar
1/3 cup best extra virgin olive oil

Make a dressing by dissolving the salt in the vinegar and then whisking in the oil. Arrange the tomatoes and onions in overlapping slices. Sprinkle with oregano and basil. Drizzle the dressing over all.

Variation: Add crumbled Gorgonzola or slices of fresh Mozzarella.

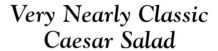

Very Nearly Classic Caesar Salad

FOR 4

Bermuda has a long-running affection for Caesar salad. The classic Caesar is made table side, and is bound by using a freshly-coddled egg. I have eliminated the *à-la-minute* aspect of the dressing (and let's face it, the dressing is the star) by coming up with a creamy version that tastes quite authentic, and can be made ahead of time.

2 egg yolks
1 1/2 cups good olive oil
1 1/2 tsp dry mustard
3 tbs wine vinegar
juice of a lemon
1 tbs Worcestershire sauce
3 cloves garlic, minced
1/2 cup grated Parmesan cheese (the real thing)
1/2 tin of anchovies, plus the oil from the tin
freshly made garlic croutons (sauté bread cubes in garlic, butter and oil until golden)
2 heads romaine lettuce (no substitutions)

In a mixer or food processor, spin the yolks until quite thickened (4 - 5 minutes). Drizzle in the oil slowly until a nice thick mayonnaise appears. Beat in most of the flavourful oil from the anchovy tin. Dissolve the mustard in the vinegar and lemon juice and beat in as well. Add the Worcestershire and the garlic. Blend in the cheese. Mash up the anchovies well and blend them in (some people don't like to actually see the little hairy fillets!) Best when chilled overnight, but you may use directly.

Tear the romaine lettuce leaves into bite-sized pieces and put in a wooden salad bowl. Pour in some dressing and toss to coat. If you need more, add to it. Toss in the croutons and decorate with additional anchovy fillets if you like.

Salamagundi

FOR 4–6

(a.k.a. Sallid Magundi and other variants.) Around since Tudor times, think of it as the British answer to France's salade Niçoise.

1 whole chicken, roasted and cooled
1 head of bibb or romaine lettuce
1/2 lb haricots verts (green beans), blanched, rinsed in cold water
1 tin of anchovy fillets
1/4 lb black, flame or green seedless grapes
4 hard-cooked eggs, quartered
12 pearl onions, blanched and peeled
1/4 cup raisins, plumped 20 minutes in warm water, drained
1 cup simple vinaigrette dressing (follows)
radish roses for garnish

Take the meat from the chicken legs and breast and slice into an appealing julienne (strips). Arrange the lettuce on a large serving platter—larger leaves as a liner, smaller leaves towards the centre. Arrange all the above elements in a most eye-appealing manner, composing them for the delectation of all. Dress the salad by drizzling the vinaigrette all over. Show everyone how pretty it is before tossing and serving.

Simple Vinaigrette

1/4 cup good red wine vinegar
salt to taste (1/4 tsp)
1/2 tsp Coleman's English Mustard
white pepper to taste
3/4 cup light olive oil
1 tbs capers, chopped
1 tsp parsley, minced

Dissolve the salt and mustard in the vinegar, then slowly drizzle in the oil, whisking constantly as you go. Add the capers, parsley and serve.

Kedgeree

FOR 4

The name comes from the Hindi, *khichri*, a dish traditionally made with rice, lentils, eggs and spices. The Anglo-Indian version, which became part of the grand British breakfast, incorporates smoked or fresh fish. I like both. Great for using up leftovers.

SIDES, SALADS & SANDWICHES

69

2 tbs butter
1 onion, chopped fine
1 clove garlic, chopped fine
1½ tbs flour
½ tsp ginger, ground
½ tsp or to taste curry powder
1 cup of milk
juice of half a lemon
1¼ cups rice, cooked with ½ tsp turmeric
8–10 oz cooked salmon, flaked
4–6 oz smoked haddock (or trout),
skinned, flaked
4 hard-cooked eggs, chopped
½ cup peas, cooked
3 tbs more or less parsley, minced
2 tbs raisins (if you have them), plumped
in warm water
salt and freshly ground pepper to taste
parsley sprigs and lemon wedges for
garnish
Major Grey's mango chutney

In a pot or pan large enough to hold all
the ingredients, sauté the onions and
garlic in the butter until translucent.
Add the flour and stir, cooking for 3–4
minutes. Add the ginger and curry
powder and begin to work in the milk
to make a smooth sauce. If too thick,
add more milk. Season with lemon
juice, salt and pepper. Add the rice and
fold in the remaining ingredients.
Adjust seasonings. When all is incorporated and well heated through,
transfer to a warmed platter, decorate

with parsley sprigs and lemon wedges
and serve good old Major Grey's
chutney alongside.

Codfish Salad

FOR 4

1 lb dried salt cod, soaked in cold water
overnight in the fridge, change once
1 small Bermuda or other sweet onion
(Walla Walla, Vidalia), chopped
2 medium tomatoes, blanched, peeled,
seeded, chopped
2 tbs good, fruity olive oil
juice of 2 limes
1 red sweet bell pepper, seeded, finely
chopped
1 hot red pepper (jalapeño, serrano,
habañero), finely chopped
1 Bermuda avocado, ripe, halved, pitted,
diced
2 cups or more mixed greens of choice

Drain and boil the cod in fresh water
to cover for 4–5 minutes, then drain,
flake and cool.

In a large non-reactive bowl, combine the fish with the onions, tomatoes, oil, lime juice (save a teaspoon's
worth), bell pepper and hot pepper and
chill.

Toss the avocado with the reserved
lime juice. Arrange the greens on
plates and mound some of the fish mixture on each. Sprinkle the avocado on

top and serve. A hibiscus blossom on each plate makes a dramatic addition.

Crab & Avocado Salad

FOR 4

1 egg yolk
2 tbs Dijon mustard
1/2 cup light olive oil
1/2 tsp Worcestershire sauce
2 tsp red wine vinegar
2 tbs chile sauce
4 green olives, chopped
salt and freshly ground pepper to taste
1 lb lump crab meat, cleaned
4 perfectly ripe avocados
romaine lettuce
1/4 cup scallions, chopped

To make the dressing whisk together the egg yolk and mustard. Drizzle in the oil, beating constantly until thick and smooth. Whisk in the Worcestershire and vinegar and more oil if a thicker dressing is desired. Add the chile sauce and olives. Season with salt and freshly ground pepper.

Mix the crab with half the dressing. Split the avocados in half, remove the pit and scoop out any brown bits. Pile dressed crab into the avocado. Place two halves of avocado on a bed of romaine, drizzle with the remaining dressing and sprinkle with scallions.

Sandwiches

Bailey's Bay Fish Sandwich

FOR 4

FOR THE BEER BATTER
one 12-oz bottle of lager
1 egg
1 egg white
12 oz (3/4 lb) flour
1 tsp baking powder
1/2 tsp salt
1/4 tsp white pepper
1/2 tsp garlic powder

Combine all the dry ingredients in a mixing bowl. Beat together the egg and egg white, add the beer, then work it into the dry mixture until well combined. Allow to rest a half hour before proceeding.

FOR THE FISH
1 cup or more vegetable oil
four 5-oz fish fillets, about 3/4-inch-thick (halibut, snapper, mahi-mahi)
salt and pepper to taste
1/2 cup flour
8 slices of bread, lightly butter on one side
8 slices Cheddar cheese
8 slices ripe tomato
tartare sauce

SIDES, SALADS & SANDWICHES

71

Heat a pot or skillet with 3 inches of oil for frying.

Lightly season the fish with salt and pepper. Dredge the fillets in flour and shake off excess. Dip each fillet in the beer batter, coat well, allow excess to drip off. Carefully lower the fillets into the hot oil and cook 4 minutes a side until golden brown. Drain on paper towels, or on a brown paper bag. While fish is cooking, grill the bread in a non-stick pan, butter side down. Top half the bread with Cheddar and tomato slices. Add the fish and top with remaining bread, cut in half and serve with tartare sauce on the side and a pitcher of rum swizzles (see Page 12).

(This recipe thanks to The Swizzle Inn)

Toasted Cheese & Bermuda Onion

FOR 4

8 slices of white bread (trimmed crusts)
16 thin slices of aged sharp Cheddar cheese (use a cheese plane)
2 Bermuda or other sweet onion (Walla Walla, Vidalia), very thinly sliced
1 tbs butter
2 tbs mayonnaise

Put 4 slices of cheese and plenty of onion between 2 slices of trimmed bread. Repeat with all sandwiches. Melt the butter in a large pan or iron skillet. Put a thin coat of mayonnaise on each sandwich and put in the hot skillet and weight down. Sauté each sandwich until golden-brown. Serve with loquat chutney (see Page 89).

AVOCADO NEGLECT

The avocado pear is abundant throughout Bermuda. It's not uncommon to see these fruit lying on the ground going to waste. The two popular types of avocado are the dark alligator-skinned Hass (rhymes with pass) and the smooth, pale-green Florida. The most common in Bermuda is the latter, ranging from fist-sized to simply gigantic. First introduced from the West Indies in 1835, avocado trees bear fruit August through February.

Avocado trees don't fruit easily unless there are suitable trees nearby which are able to fertilise them.

One of nature's most nutrient-packed foods, the avocado is more than just for codfish breakfast and guacamole. A happy addition to any salad, fruit or savoury, it's also a tasty snack doused with Crazy Jane's Mixed Up Salt, mashed and spread on bread, or used as a salsa (with tomatoes, scallions, hot peppers, cilantro, lime juice and salt).

Tuna Salad on a 'Coffee Roll'

Bermudians are fond of having tuna salad (a codfish cake or other fillings) served on a sugar-iced "coffee roll," what you may call a Danish. It sound strange, but actually it's a rather tasty, if messy, sandwich. Also good on an English muffin or toasted scone.

one 7-oz tin of chunk tuna in water or oil
2 (or more) tbs mayonnaise (Bermudians
are among the highest consumers of mayo-
nnaise per capita in the world)
$^1\!/_2$ medium Bermuda onion or other sweet
onion (Walla Walla, Vidalia), minced .
1 rib celery, minced
2 tsp fresh thyme leaves
Tabasco, or other hot sauce to taste
(optional)
salt, freshly ground pepper to taste

2 warmed "coffee rolls," sliced lengthwise

Drain the tuna well and, with a fork, blend with the mayonnaise. Add all the remaining ingredients and blend well. Adjust seasonings with salt, pepper and Tabasco. Spread thickly on a warmed coffee roll and enjoy.

Ferry Reach Sandwich Loaf

Dinghy races are a Bermuda tradition. Non-competitors love to watch from their boats—a perfect, easy lunch to take along.

1 long crusty French loaf
1 lb fresh spinach, washed and stemmed
4 ripe tomatoes, sliced and pressed gently
on a paper towel
1 large tin tuna in olive oil
freshly ground black pepper
2 Bermuda onions, thinly sliced
6 hard-cooked eggs, sliced
1 tin anchovies
10 cornichons, sliced lengthwise
1 tbs Dijon mustard
1 tbs mayonnaise

Slice the bread in half lengthwise and scoop out some of the soft middle. Drizzle the oil from the tuna tin on the bottom half of the bread. Put down a layer of spinach, then tomatoes. Now sprinkle in the tuna and grind some pepper on top. Top this with rings of onion and a layer of sliced eggs, topped here and there with anchovy fillets and pickles. Put a thin smear of mustard and a thinner smear of mayonnaise on the top half of the loaf and press it down gently, but firmly, on the loaded bottom. Wrap in a long length of foil. When ready, cut through the foil and hand out a section to each sailor.

SIDES,
SALADS &
SANDWICHES

Cooking Outdoors

Cooking Outdoors

In Bermuda, nearly everyone I know has some sort of outdoor grill: a table-top hibachi, or a huge converted half oil drum; a run-of-the-mill coal kettle grill or a gas and lava rock grill. A few have elaborate domed, two-tiered, gas-fired consoles with hot plates, temperature gauges, utensil holsters and cutting boards that are a veritable kitchen and entertainment centre on wheels. Bermudians love to play and cook out-doors, and can do it year round.

Gas-fired grills are very convenient and popular, but I still favour the characteristic flavour that comes from using charcoal briquettes. If you choose this 'old-fashioned' method, be sure to light the coals at least 20 minutes before you want to begin cooking.

For charcoal grills, there are a variety of starters: electric (but that means extension cords), little metal, chimney-shaped containers into which you pile the coals for 'easy' lighting (a bit of a complex contrivance), liquid fuels (no matter what they say, these leave some lingering 'perfume'), and light-in-the-bag options. Old reliable wadded paper, kindling and a match or two usually work quite well. Of course, if you have a gas grill, it's as easy as turning on the range. Gas grills should be allowed to pre-heat for 10 to 15 minutes.

Once you've got the coals going, muster some patience. They are hot when covered with a thin white ash beneath which you detect a ruddy glow. If you want more heat, tap off some of the ash with a stick.

Aromatic wood chips continue to be popular. Mesquite, a fairly pungent wood, has enjoyed deserved popularity, but chips of hickory, grape vine pieces, and oak (especially good with beef and chicken), maple and apple woods (tasty with lamb), can also add delightful nuances. Store-bought wood bits last longer and do their smoky best when soaked in water for a half-hour. Toss other flavouring agents like fresh rosemary, thyme, or fennel on the fire, keeping in mind what best complements what you're cooking.

Before the food hits the heat, brush the grill with a little vegetable oil to prevent sticking. It is always better to use tongs than a meat-piercing fork, which allows precious juices to escape.

TOOLS TO HAVE ON HAND I find three items are essential: tongs, a basting brush and a plant spritzer to douse inevitable flare-ups. A hinged wire grill basket comes in handy to keep vegetables and such from falling into the fire. A metal spatula is useful with burgers and fish. It's not a bad idea to have some sort of drip pan in or under your grill. And don't forget to keep a pitcher of Dark 'n Stormies at hand to add to the festive spirit.

GRILL TIMES

A moderate grill is about 400 degrees. With beef or lamb, do the finger test for doneness: medium-rare should feel like pinching the soft flesh by the crook in your arm. If this is too inaccurate, cut the meat and peek for pinkness.

Chicken breast (boneless)	15 minutes
Chicken quarters	45–50 minutes, turn frequently
Steaks and chops	6 minutes per inch for rare
	8 for medium-rare
	10 for medium
4 lbs of baby back ribs	1–1½ hours, turn frequently
4 lbs spare ribs (not blanched)	1 hour, turn frequently
1–2 lb flank steak	12–15 minutes, turn once
Meat kebabs	20 minutes, lid open
Fish kebabs	10-12 minutes, lid open
Sausages	12–15 minutes, turn frequently

Whole roasts take about the same time as they would in the oven: 15 minutes per pound for rare, 20 minutes for medium with the lid down.

If you have an instant reading thermometer:
for beef, lamb and game
140 degrees rare
150 degrees medium
160 degrees well-done
for pork or veal
150 degrees in the centre is just fine

77

Burgers

Blues Burger

FOR *4*

1½ lbs ground beef (lean, not chuck)
2 tbs unsalted butter, softened
⅓ cup Danish blue cheese, crumbled
*6 strips of bacon, cooked crispy, drained
and broken into bits*
alfalfa sprouts
salt and pepper to taste
English muffins

Mash together the butter and blue cheese and put in a bowl or form into a log and put in the fridge to harden up (may be made days ahead, if you wish).

Make four burgers with the ground beef, handling them as little as possible. Season with salt and pepper and grill over medium hot coals about 5–6 minutes on each side for medium-rare. Overcooking will give you a dry result. Serve on grill-toasted English muffins, arrange Roquefort butter, crumbled bacon bits and alfalfa sprouts in pots for burger-maker's assembly.

Goat Cheese Burger

FOR *4*

1½ lb ground lamb
salt and freshly ground pepper to taste
2 oz cream cheese
2 oz goat cheese
2 scallions, minced
*1–2 hot peppers jalapeño, serrano,
habañero, stemmed, seeded, chopped*
1 tsp cilantro, chopped

Combine the ground lamb and the salt and pepper and form into 8 patties. Handle the burgers as little as possible.

Mix together the cream cheese and goat cheese with the scallions, hot peppers and cilantro. Spread this mixture over 4 of the patties. Now top these with the remaining 4 patties, making sandwiches; press together around the edges trapping the filling inside.

Grill over medium hot coals about 6 minutes on each side for medium-rare. Overcooking will give you a dry result. Serve in pita pockets with Hot Mango 'Ketchup' (see Page 88).

COOKING
OUTDOORS

Meat, Poultry & Fish

Butterflied Lamb with Citrus Rum Marinade

FOR 6

7–8-lb leg of lamb, boned and butterflied
½ cup good olive oil
½ cup of fresh orange juice
juice of one lime
¼ cup Gosling's Black Seal Rum
3–4 cloves of garlic, smashed
1 tsp of dried mint
2 tsp cumin
1–2 bay leaves, broken into pieces
1 heaping tbs fresh parsley, minced
1 tsp of coarse salt (or to taste)
freshly ground black pepper to taste

Trim the lamb of any excess fat and membrane. If there is a great disparity in the thickness of the lamb overall, separate into 2 pieces and cook one a little less. Combine the oil, juices, Gosling's Black Seal Rum garlic, mint, cumin, bay leaves, parsley, ground pepper and a half-teaspoon of salt in a shallow glass or glazed bowl or pan. Marinate the lamb for 3–4 hours at room temperature or overnight in the refrigerator.

Once the fire is at its peak, brush the grill with oil and sear the lamb well on each side. Remove from the heat, season with the remaining salt and let the meat rest for 10 minutes. Then grill the lamb an additional 20–25 minutes, basting frequently and turning once after half

BURGER BASICS

• When forming the patties, wet your hands with water and handle the meat as little as possible. If necessary, make into a quick ball and then form between sheets of cling wrap. The enzymes in our skin dry and toughen the meat.
• Brush some oil on the grill rack before cooking to prevent sticking.
• Cook over a moderate heat. A blackened burger, unless it has Cajun pretensions, is not a taste treat.
• Don't keep pressing the burger as it cooks—it pushes out the very juices you want to keep in. If you want something to do while you stand at the grill, try a Dark 'n Stormy!
• Have all condiments and garnish laid out in little bowls and dishes before you start cooking. Invite your guests to assemble their burgers.
• Don't be afraid to serve an extraordinary wine with a burger.
• General rule: Never turn your back on the grill.

COOKING
OUTDOORS

79

the time has elapsed. Keep an eye out for excessive charring. Raise the grill a notch if you feel it's approaching the blackened stage. Slice the medium-rare lamb crosswise on the diagonal as you would a flank steak or a London broil—thinly and against the grain. Serve with grilled vegetables.

Rum 'n Spicy Flank Steak

FOR 6

2 lbs flank steak

FOR THE MARINADE
1/4 cup olive oil
3 tbs lime juice
1 clove garlic, minced
2 tbs or so cilantro (optional)
1 tsp cumin
2 tbs Gosling's Black Seal Rum
1 tsp or to taste chile powder
1 jalapeño pepper, minced

Put all ingredients in a sealed plastic bag. Marinate 3 hours or overnight in the refrigerator. Grill or broil the marinated flank steak until rare (8–12 minutes, turning once). Allow a few minutes before cutting thinly on the diagonal. Simple and tasty.

COOKING
OUTDOORS

Black Seal Rum Steaks With Sweet Mustard Sauce

FOR 4

four 1 1/2-inch porterhouse or rib-eye steaks
1/4 cup sweet mustard
1/4 cup Gosling's Black Seal Rum
3–4 medium shallots, minced
salt and freshly ground black pepper to taste

Mix together the mustard, Gosling's Black Seal Rum and shallots. Salt and pepper the steaks and coat generously with the mixture. Let stand a half-hour at room temperature, or in the refrigerator up to 2 hours. Oil the rack and sear the steak 2 minutes on each side, basting once. Put down the lid and cook 3 minutes on each side for rare. Serve with any remaining basting sauce.

Nice served with skewered cherry tomatoes, brushed with olive oil and grilled for 5 minutes.

Spanish Point Ribs

FOR 4

6 lbs of spare ribs or baby back ribs
1 recipe Rum Fire & Brimstone Rib Sauce (see 'Vhat Goes Vith,' Page 87)

Blanch the ribs in boiling water for 15 minutes. Generously baste both sides of the rack with the sauce.

Prepare the grill. When the coals are hot, oil the grill rack and place the ribs on the grill cooking over a moderate heat for 5–7 minutes. Turn and baste, grilling and basting until done—another 10 or so minutes. Test for doneness— don't overcook. Serve with additional sauce for dipping.

Rummy-Peach Country-Style Pork Ribs

FOR 6

6 lbs country-style (thick cut) pork ribs
1 recipe Peach Barbecue Glaze (see 'Vhat Goes Vith,' Page 88)

Coat the ribs with plenty of the peach barbecue glaze. Be sure the grill is at the highest distance from the flames or that the gas is on the lowest setting—we want to slow-cook these darlings. Place the ribs on the well-oiled grill and cook on one side for 20 minutes, then turn, coating the cooked side anew with glaze. Turn again in 20 minutes, coat with glaze and test for doneness. If they need a few more minutes, mop with glaze and continue cooking. The ribs should be cooked through, but not to death.

Black Seal-Barbecued Chicken

FOR 4

The variations on barbecued chicken are endless. Everyone has a favourite sauce they feel is the best. I like to keep up the search.

one 4-lb chicken, cut in eighths

FOR THE BASTING SAUCE
1/2 red onion, minced
1 tbs olive oil
1/2 cup ketchup
2 tsp Worcestershire sauce
1 tsp cider vinegar
1 tsp chile powder
1/2 tsp cayenne pepper or to taste
1/4 cup Gosling's Black Seal Rum
1 tsp sherry peppers or other hot sauce

Remove any excess fat from the chicken, rinse and pat dry. When the fire is hot, place the chicken on an oiled grill, skin side down and, when well seared, turn over. Cook for a half-hour, over slow heat, before beginning to baste with the sauce. Turn once, baste, then turn again. Continue basting, but not turning, until cooked through another 20–30 minutes. Be careful not to char the chicken.

During the initial cooking time, or well in advance, you may prepare the

COOKING
OUTDOORS

THE PORTUGUESE IN BERMUDA

During the Age of Discovery, the Spanish and Portuguese were Britain's biggest competitors. Long before the British decided to settle Bermuda, Spanish and Portuguese explorers had sighted, landed or been wrecked on Bermuda's reefs. In Sebastian Cabot's 1544 *Mappa Mundi*, Bermuda was listed as The Isle of Devils, so treacherous was the ring of reefs surrounding it and the myths generated by the mounting list of tragedies.

The first Portuguese to settle in Bermuda came long after the glories of Portuguese exploration by Vasco da Gama and Pedro Cabral. In November, 1849, a group of 58 immigrants, men, women and children, arrived from Madeira. Many more would come, and still do, from the Açores, a verdant, nine-island archipelago in the mid-Atlantic. The Portuguese were instrumental in building Bermuda's ability to produce vegetables and fruits for export markets on the US Eastern Seaboard during the 19th and 20th centuries. Over the years, they, like most immigrants, assimilated in many ways, but thankfully never gave up their foods. Red bean soup, spicy chouriço sausages, octopus stew, codfish, fava bean stew, sweet eggbread, buscotos, malaçadas (a type of doughnut), and other sweets, together with herb-rich cuisine using thyme, rosemary, kale, and garlic, are among the distinctive dishes and cross-cultural influences that have become part of Bermudian cooking.

Today, Portuguese-Bermudians, making up 10 percent of the local population, are Members of Parliament, doctors and lawyers, business executives, landscapers, gardeners, and many still farm the land.

For recipes for dishes mentioned, see the Recipe Index, Pages 129–132.

COOKING
OUTDOORS

Chouriço on the Grill

Locally-made chouriço sausage, a Portuguese speciality, pronounced "shah-deesh," is garlicky, spicy and a real treat. To prepare it on the grill is simplicity itself. First, buy the best, leanest, hottest you can find. Prick the skin and place over moderate heat. Allow to cook, turning frequently and pricking occasionally, until well-browned, even black on some spots. Enjoy with coleslaw or potato salad on a plate, or put it in a crusty hoagie bun which you have heated on the grill. Have a nice, ice-cold bottle of your favourite brew handy.

sauce. You can do this in a pot on the grill while the chicken is cooking. Sauté the onion in the olive oil until softened. Add the remaining ingredients and bring to a boil. Simmer 20 minutes, taking care it doesn't get too thick.

Three-Citrus Chicken

FOR 4

4 large chicken breasts, split, boned (or 8 thighs)
1/4 cup light olive oil
juice of 2 fresh limes
juice of an orange
juice of a lemon
1/4 cup Gosling's Black Seal Rum
2 cloves garlic, minced
2 jalapeño or serrano peppers, seeded, chopped
1/4 tsp salt
freshly ground white pepper to taste
slices of lime, orange and lemon for garnish

Combine the oil, juices, Gosling's Black Seal Rum, garlic and peppers in a shallow baking dish. Marinate the chicken in a baking dish at room temperature for 1 hour or overnight in the refrigerator, turning once. Remove the chicken from the marinade, season with white pepper. In a blender, combine the marinade, including the hot peppers and liquefy. Brush the breasts well with the pepper basting sauce.

Cook on an oiled grill for 7 or 8 minutes per side (10–12 minutes for thighs) basting constantly. Garnish with overlapping slices of each citrus.

Cedar-Planked Salmon

Bermuda was once forested with cedar.

FOR 6

3 1/2–4 lb whole salmon fillet
1 natural (untreated) cedar plank 2 x 6 x 18 inches soaked in water several hours
1/4 cup ginger, minced

FOR THE SPICE RUB
1 tbs nutmeg
1 tbs allspice
1 tbs cardamom
1 tbs white pepper
1 tsp salt
1/4 cup packed light brown sugar

Put the well-soaked plank on the hot grill and close the lid, allowing the plank to heat up. Meanwhile, score the salmon deeply, diagonally, like a holiday ham. Mix together the rub ingredients. Sprinkle the ginger into the cuts and then rub all over with the spice mixture (save any extra). Slip the salmon on to the now smoking plank and cook lid-down for about 20 minutes or until just done at the centre. The plank may be re-used a few times.

COOKING
OUTDOORS

Grilled Amberjack

FOR 2

Amberfish is locally known as "jack." A firm-fleshed fish, abundant in our waters, it can be mighty delicious.

juice of a lemon
¼ cup Gosling's Rum Deluxe
¼ cup light olive oil
salt and freshly ground pepper to taste
2 whole amberjacks, gutted and scaled
several sprigs of fresh rosemary
lemon wedges

Mix together the lemon juice, rum, olive oil, salt and pepper. Dip and coat the fish well and let marinate while the coals get hot. Put some rosemary in the cavity and sprinkle some on the fish. Grill five minutes per side or until just done—peek at the bone. Garnish with rosemary sprigs and lemon wedges.

Grog-Grilled Tuna

FOR 4

four 2-inch-thick Bermuda tuna steaks
juice of 2 limes
4 tbs Goslings Black Seal Rum
1 tsp soy sauce
1 tsp ginger, grated
lime wedges for garnish

While the coals are getting hot, sit the tuna steaks in the lime juice, Gosling's

Black Seal Rum, soy and ginger for 20 minutes or so. Grill the fish 3–4 inches from the heat. When browned (about 4 minutes) turn and cook another 4–5 minutes. Check for doneness, should be just opaque in the middle. Don't overcook. Serve immediately with lime wedges.

Seafood & Melon Kebabs

FOR 4

1 lb large shrimp peeled, deveined, tails on
1 lb sea scallops, muscle removed
1 large cantaloupe, scooped with the large end of a melon-baller
juice of 2 oranges
¼ cup Gosling's Black Seal Rum
1 tbs fresh ginger, minced
1 tbs jalapeño or serrano pepper, minced
¼ cup peanut oil
salt and freshly ground pepper to taste

Marinate the shrimp and scallops in the orange juice, Gosling's Black Seal Rum, ginger, pepper and oil for 30 minutes. Thread the seafood, alternating shrimp, scallops and melon, on pre-soaked bamboo skewers (to prevent scorching). Season with salt and pepper and grill over hot coals about 2 minutes a side until just cooked. Brush during cooking with leftover marinade. Serve hot.

'Vhat Goes Vith'

It's not a proper cookout without coleslaw, potato and macaroni salads. Here they are—and a few more—dishes that 'go with.'

Coleslaw

FOR A SMALL CROWD

¹/₂ head of green cabbage, sliced for coleslaw
¹/₂ head red cabbage, sliced for coleslaw
4 large carrots, peeled then sliced with peeler into curls or finely jullienned
¹/₄ cup raisins, plumped in a Dark 'n Stormy (Page 12), drained
1 tbs toasted sesame seeds
1 tbs poppy seeds

FOR THE DRESSING
³/₄ cup mayonnaise
¹/₃ cup sour cream
3 tbs Dijon mustard
¹/₄ cup apple cider vinegar
3 dashes wine vinegar peppers

Mix together the mayonnaise and the sour cream. Now add the mustard, and finally the vinegar and vinegar peppers. Toss together the cabbages, carrots, raisins (drink the Dark 'n Stormy), sesame and poppy seeds—then dress using only enough to coat well, not swamp, the veggies. Better if it stands overnight in the fridge.

Potato Salad

FOR A SMALL CROWD

This potato salad is more complex than the garden variety of boiled potatoes and jarred mayonnaise.

3 lbs red potatoes, scrubbed, skin on
¹/₄ cup dry vermouth
2 tbs grainy Dijon mustard
¹/₃ cup peanut oil
¹/₃ cup apple cider vinegar
2 tsp Tabasco, or other Louisiana-style hot sauce
2 garlic cloves, minced
2 tsp celery seed
sea salt and freshly ground pepper to taste
4 oz or more Stilton cheese
2 tbs fresh parsley, minced

Put the potatoes in a large pot with cold water to cover. Bring to a boil and cook until fork tender (a half-hour or less). Drain and cool under cold running water just enough so you can comfortably handle them. Cut the larger potatoes in half, even quarters. Toss with the vermouth and allow to continue to cool down.

   Make a dressing by whisking together

COOKING
OUTDOORS

85

the mustard and oil, then the vinegar, hot sauce, garlic, celery seed, salt and pepper. Pour on and blend with the potatoes. Crumble the cheese all over and sprinkle with parsley and fold in gently. Keep cool. Best served the same day.

Macaroni Salad

FOR 6

Another variation on a standard. My favourite—so far.

1 lb small shell macaroni, cooked in plenty of well-salted water, drained and 'refreshed' with cold water
3/4 cup mayonnaise
1/4 cup sour cream
1 tbs Dijon mustard
2 tbs fresh dill, minced
sherry peppers, or your favourite hot sauce, to taste
salt to taste
2 cloves garlic, minced
1 cup radish, cut in matchsticks
1 cup corn frozen, blanched or freshly cooked, cob cut off
1 small red bell pepper, chopped
1 small yellow bell pepper, chopped
cayenne pepper to taste

Mix together the mayonnaise, sour cream, mustard, dill, sherry peppers, salt and garlic. Toss together the macaroni, radish matchsticks, corn and

COOKING
OUTDOORS

sweet peppers. Dress gently, adding mayonnaise and sour cream as desired and chill overnight in the refrigerator to allow flavours to develop. Adjust seasonings before serving at just cooler than room temperature.

Miss Peg's Egg Salad

FOR 6

Once again, scrumptious liberties have been taken with the classic recipe.

8 eggs, hard-boiled, chopped coarsely
1 medium onion, minced
2 ribs celery, sliced thinly
1 bunch watercress, stems removed, chopped
2–3 tbs parsley, minced

FOR THE DRESSING
1/2 cup mayonnaise
1/4 cup sour cream
1 tbs good curry powder
1 tsp fresh lemon juice
salt and white pepper to taste
paprika for garnish

Toss together the eggs, onion, celery, watercress and parsley, reserving a little for garnish. Mix together the mayonnaise, sour cream, curry and lemon juice. Dress the egg mixture by carefully folding in the dressing until well-coated. Refrigerate until ready to enjoy. Sprinkle with paprika before serving.

Banana Beauty 'Ketchup'

1 cup water
1 cup apple cider vinegar
1/3 cup molasses
1/4 cup honey
3 ripe Bermuda strawberry bananas, mashed
1/4 tomato paste
1 medium Bermuda onion, minced
2–3 cloves garlic, minced
1–2 hot peppers (jalapeño, serrano, habañero), stemmed, seeded
1/3 cup raisins
1 tsp salt
1 tsp cinnamon
1/4 teaspoon allspice
1/4 teaspoon nutmeg
1/8 tsp ground cloves
6–8 turns on the peppermill
1/4 cup Gosling's Black Seal Rum

Heat the water, vinegar, molasses, honey, bananas and tomato paste, stirring until blended. Add the onions, garlic, hot peppers, raisins and simmer 5 minutes. Add the spices and Gosling's Black Seal Rum and simmer another 20 minutes until syrupy. Purée roughly by pulsing in a blender or food processor. Great with grilled fish, meat or fowl.

Rum, Fire & Brimstone Barbecue Sauce

one 6-oz tin tomato paste
1/4 cup molasses
3 tbs brown sugar
1/2 cup Gosling's Black Seal Rum
3 cloves garlic
generous pinch of allspice
2 tbs Worcestershire sauce
2 tbs soy sauce
4–6 jalapeño, serrano or habañero peppers seeded, chopped

Combine all ingredients in a food processor and pulse until smooth. Pour into a heavy-bottomed pot and bring to a boil. Simmer 2 minutes and remove from flame. Cool completely and cover in a snap lid jar. If refrigerated, it will keep for months. Very hot on the tongue, nearly tolerable when cooked.

COOKING
OUTDOORS

GRILLED FRUIT A nice, often unexpected, accompaniment to grilled meats. Merely brush some peaches, nectarines, plums, apples or pears with light olive oil and roll them around in a not too hot corner of the grill. Peaches, nectarines and plums take about 10 minutes to soften and heat through; apples and pears about twice as long.

Hot Mango 'Ketchup'

2 tbs light olive oil
1 medium red onion, finely chopped
1/2 cup apple cider vinegar
1/2 cup light brown sugar
1/4 cup molasses
3 ripe mangoes, peeled, pitted, chunked
2–3 hot peppers (jalapeño, serrano, habañero), seeded, chopped
salt and freshly ground pepper to taste

Sauté the onions in the oil until golden. Add the vinegar, sugar, molasses, mango and hot peppers and bring to a boil. Simmer for 1 hour until thickened. Purée in the blender, or leave chunky as you desire. Refrigerate until ready to use. Keeps about 2 weeks.

Peach Barbecue Glaze

Wild peaches grow all over Bermuda.

1/2 cup unsalted butter
1/2 tsp each basil, mace and nutmeg
2 tsp more of less of salt
2 tbs brown sugar
2 cups puréed peaches, tinned, or fresh, peeled and pitted
4 tbs frozen orange juice concentrate
2 tbs fresh lemon juice
4 tbs Gosling's Black Seal Rum

In a heavy-bottomed pot, melt the butter and add the spices, salt and sugar, stirring until combined. Now add the purée, juices and rum. Blend until smooth and cook about 5 minutes until thickened. Use as a mop for grilling chicken or pork. You may use first as a marinade.

Sweet-Patootie Ribs 'n Chicken Sauce

2 cups minced Bermuda or other sweet onion
2–3 garlic cloves, minced
1 tbs peanut oil
1 tbs fresh ginger, minced
1 tsp Coleman's English Mustard
1 cup ketchup
3/4 cup Bermuda honey
1/4 cup Worcestershire sauce
1/4 cup Goslings Black Seal Rum
1/4 cup apple cider vinegar

Sauté the onions in the oil until translucent, add the garlic and cook until the onions go golden. Stir in the remaining ingredients in the order of appearance. Simmer for a half-hour, or until thickened. Keeps well, tastes great with grilled chicken or pork ribs. Yields just over 1 1/2 cups.

Loquat Chutney

5 cups loquats, stemmed and stoned
2 large onions, chopped fine
1 clove garlic, chopped
1 Granny Smith apple, peeled, chopped
1¹/₂ cup dried cranberries, plumped in warm water
2 oz ginger root, peeled, minced
4 cups brown sugar
1 lime cut in eighths, blanched in boiling water
1 tsp salt
1 tsp cloves
1 tsp allspice
1 tsp nutmeg
¹/₄ cup apple cider vinegar
¹/₂ cup walnuts (optional)

Combine all ingredients except the walnuts in a heavy-bottomed pot and slowly bring to a boil. Simmer until thickened. Remove from heat. Add optional walnuts. Ladle into very clean snap-lid containers leaving a half-inch head room. Label and date. Keeps 3–4 weeks refrigerated. Great with chicken, turkey, pork, game, or just on cream cheese and crackers.

Sue & Nigel's Excellent Tomato Chutney

Bermuda tomatoes are superb, thin-skinned, vine-ripened.

10 large dried hot red chiles, soaked, seeded
2 oz ginger root
2 tsp turmeric
6 tsp cumin seeds
¹/₄ cup vegetable oil
10 garlic cloves, peeled, crushed
1 cup sugar
2 tbs salt
1 cup apple cider vinegar
4 lbs firm red tomatoes cut in eighths

In a blender, grind together the chiles, ginger, turmeric and cumin seeds with a tablespoon's worth of the oil. Heat the remaining oil in a heavy-bottomed pan and stir in the spices for about a minute to heat them through. Reduce the heat, add the garlic, and cook until translucent. Add the sugar, salt and vinegar. Once the sugar has dissolved, add the tomatoes. Cook slowly, stirring occasionally until the tomatoes are soft and pulpy. It takes a while—be patient. Cool completely, then spoon into very clean jars. Seal, label and date.

COOKING
OUTDOORS

Good Friday

Codfish Cakes & Hot Cross Buns

Visitors coming to Bermuda for the Easter weekend will be in for an amusing surprise on Good Friday. This holy day of grim and solemn significance on the Christian calender, is celebrated by flying brightly-coloured homemade kites, playing marbles and eating codfish cakes and hot cross buns.

The sky fills with kites ranging from the small and simple to elaborate colourful hexagons and three-dimensional geometrics that resemble models of complex chemical crystals. Bermuda's best-known beach, Horseshoe Bay, is the most popular spot for kite contests, games and activities. As the day wears on, the beach becomes thick with children and adults all looking upward, all tugging, like fisherman, on lines cast into an ocean of sky.

Some say the origin of this tradition began when a Sunday school teacher used a simple cross-stick kite with the image of Jesus on it to illustrate the Ascension. Once the kite was aloft, the string was cut and the heaven-bound kite drifted until it was a dot upon the sky, and then disappeared.

Good Friday also means codfish cakes and hot 'cross' buns. The latter date from the time of Pope Gregory I, of calendar fame (600 A.D.). Flavoured with cinnamon and allspice with plumped raisins throughout, they are a borrowed British tradition. In the 16th century, bakers were forbidden from making any spice cakes or buns except at burials, the Friday before Easter and Christmas, "upon paine of forfeiture of all such breads to the poor." A cross is applied with white icing sugar, then the bun is glazed. "Good Friday comes this month," went the 18th-century ditty. "The old women runs with one, or two-a-penny hot cross buns. Whose virtue is, if you believe what's said, they'll not grow mouldy like common bread."

Codfish has even older origins. Fish has always been a part of the ancient iconography of the Christian Church. Early Coptic Christians used the Greek word for fish, *icthus*, to serve as an anagram for the phrase "Jesus Christ, Son of God, Saviour."

Codfish cakes made from well-soaked salt cod, combined with cooked potatoes, fresh thyme, parsley and onion, dusted with flour or breadcrumbs and fried golden are served throughout the day. With a hot cross bun, or in the bun, they are a tasty tradition.

BERMUDA
TRADITIONS

92

Hot Cross Buns

2½ lbs flour
2 packets active dry yeast
3 oz brown sugar
3 cups warm water
2½ lbs unsalted butter
2 large eggs
2 tbs cinnamon
½ tbs allspice
½ tsp salt
1 lb raisins

FOR THE CROSS
1 cup warm water
1 cup (or a little more) flour
½ tsp salt

FOR THE GLAZE
2½ cups sugar
1¼ cups water
¾ cup light corn syrup

Mix together the yeast, water and sugar and set aside a few minutes until the yeast starts to foam. Mix together the flour, spices and salt.

With a mixer or by hand, mix the flour, eggs and butter into the yeast-water mixture. Now add the raisins. The dough will be somewhat sticky, but should pull away from the sides of the bowl and form a ball. If not, add a little more flour. Cover with a towel and let it rest in a warm place until it doubles in bulk. Be sure it is in a bowl large enough to accommodate its new size.

Punch down the dough and cut into small 2½-ounce pieces (you don't have to weigh it—just eyeball it). Roll into a ball and place on a baking sheet several inches part. When all are lined up, cover again with a towel and put in a warm place away from draughts and allow to rise for 15–20 minutes. You will need more than one baking sheet.

Preheat the oven to 400 degrees.

While waiting, make the 'crosses' by mixing together the flour, water and salt so it's thick enough to pipe through a pastry bag fitted with a small round tip about an inch in diameter. Pipe a cross on each risen bun. Bake at 400 degrees for about 15–20 minutes or until golden.

While the buns are baking, make the glaze by boiling together the sugar, water and corn syrup over moderate heat until the sugar is completely dissolved. When it looks clear, brush down the sides with a pastry brush dipped in cold water. Allow to cool. It will be sticky but still "brushable."

When the buns emerge from the oven, cool on the rack and brush with glaze.

(This recipe is from Crow Lane Bakery)

BERMUDA
TRADITIONS

93

Codfish Cakes

MAKES ABOUT 10, DEPENDING ON SIZE

1 lb salt cod
3 large potatoes, boiled as for mashing
1 tbs Dijon mustard and 1 tbs mayonnaise, mixed
1 tbs fresh ginger root, minced
2 cloves garlic, minced
3 tbs fresh thyme (more if you like)
several dashes of sherry peppers sauce or to taste
1 cup seasoned breadcrumbs
vegetable oil for frying
2 large bananas

Soak the cod overnight, changing the water at least once.

In fresh water, bring the cod to a boil and cook until the fish is tender and flaky (8 minutes). Do not overcook. Drain well and cool.

Mash together the cod and potatoes. Add the thyme, ginger, garlic and the mustard mayonnaise.

Roll into balls the size of a lemon. Flatten and press into the breadcrumbs. Fry until golden. Top with a slice of banana and serve with, or in, hot cross buns.

BERMUDA
TRADITIONS

Cup Match

Cup Match, more than mere cricket rivalry and only slightly removed from a circus, is a lot more than wickets and overs. But when all is said and done, it pretty much resembles the event from which it evolved—a giant picnic.

Some historians claim cricket matches were already in full swing, so to speak, between the Royal Navy and the British garrison as early as 1846. Others credit a certain Captain J. Moresby for having introduced the game at a carnival in Somerset in 1872. Whatever the actual date, black Bermudians imitated the uppercrustic sport with rustic bats and balls fashioned from cloth-wound rocks. By 1890, the formation of an all-black Bermuda Militia Artillery made the procurement of proper cricket gear possible, and black Bermudians officially joined in the matches.

Turn-of-the-century clubs from Pride of India Lodge of St. George's, and the Grand United Order of Odd Fellows Lodge of Somerset would play against one another at the annual Emancipation Day picnic. It was all good fun and good food. And, of course, good cricket. As the years progressed, so did the seriousness of the rivalry. After a hotly-contested match in 1901, they decided the following year they'd play for a cup.

A collection was taken up, not to

exceed sixpence per contributor, to be put towards a silver trophy. The first Cup Match, in 1902, was between the new Somerset Cricket Club and St. George's Cricket Club established in 1892. Ever since, St. George's stalwarts have displayed the navy and light-blue ribbons, and the Somerset supporters sport the red and blue colours.

Forty-two years later, Somers (Founder's) Day and Emancipation Day were tacked on to the first August week-end, making Cup Match a much-antici-pated four-day celebration. By mid-July, you begin to see partisan colours emerge, flying from car aerials. The biggest question is: *"Vhat you vearin' to Cup Metch?"* (Smart shoppers buy a size larger than what they're wearing to accommodate the feasting to come.)

Folks move into the stands and stake their claim. 'Skyboxes' are built, tarpaulins go up, coolers are arranged, and under a big tent, 'Crown & Anchor' gaming tables are set up. (This is legal illegal gambling and Bermudians love it.) It is said that tens of millions of dollars are withdrawn from banks in the days before Cup Match and are redeposited, in different accounts, the Monday after.

In spite of broiling midsummer heat, the most sought-after foods are conch stew, fish chowder, mussel and beef pies, codfish cakes, fish and chips, fried chicken, and barbecued ribs. Old-time

Cup Matchers start the day with conch stew for breakfast!

According to veteran Cup Match food vendor and St. David's Islander, Dolly Pitcher, "people go to Cup Match for four reasons—the food, Crown & Anchor, drinking, and (after a long pause) the cricket," she says laughing.

Curried Mussel Pie

Bermudians love some mussel pie at Cup Match and anytime of the year. The local custom is to have the lid of the hot pie sliced open and a dollop of mayonnaise inserted.

FOR THE PIE FILLING
¼ bushel small mussels, scrubbed
2 lbs potatoes, cut in small dice
2 medium onions, chopped fine
2 tbs fresh thyme
1 tbs parsley, minced
2 tbs curry powder
1 tbs Worcestershire sauce
1 tsp gravy browning
salt and pepper to taste
¼ cup water
3 tbs cornstarch

Steam the mussels in ¾ cup of water and reserve the broth. Remove the mus-sels from their shells and keep ready. Strain the broth of all grit (a fine strainer or cheesecloth should be used) and re-heat. Boil the onions, potatoes,

BERMUDA
TRADITIONS

thyme and parsley together in the water until the potatoes are tender. Add the curry powder, Worcestershire sauce, gravy browning, and mussels and bring to a boil. Thicken with cornstarch mixed with cold water, added while mixture is boiling. If it's not thick enough, repeat with more cornstarch and water. Allow the filling to cool before proceeding.

FOR THE PASTRY
2 cups flour
1 tsp salt
2/3 cup cold vegetable shortening
1/4 cup iced water

Stir together the flour and the salt. Cut the shortening into the flour in stages until it resembles small peas. Sprinkle with a little water and toss to moisten the dough. Work the dough as little as possible, using as few strokes as you can to get it all combined into a ball of dough. Flatten slightly and wrap with plastic wrap, and chill for at least an hour or up to 4 days in the refrigerator (a month in the freezer). Let dough soften at room temperature before rolling out. Use the inverted pie pan or ramekin to measure the circle of dough needed. Fill pans or ramekins, cut and fit dough to top of pie. Bake until golden-brown and bubbly within.

Conch Stew

1/4 lb salt pork, cut in small dice
2 large Bermuda onions, chopped
3 lbs conch meat, pounded to tenderise, cut in dice
1 cup water
2 large carrots, diced
3 potatoes, diced
3 sprigs of fresh thyme
3 sprigs of fresh parsley
2 tbs butter
2 tbs flour
1/4 cup Gosling's Black Seal Rum
2 tbs ketchup
1 tbs Worcestershire sauce
1 tsp wine vinegar
freshly ground black pepper and Tabasco to taste

Sauté the salt pork until it has rendered most of its fat. Add the onions and cook until golden. Add the conch meat and a cup of water and simmer until tender. Add the vegetables and herbs and simmer until they are just tender. In another pot, combine the butter and flour to make a *roux*. Cook over a moderate heat until it turns a caramel colour. Strain a little of the broth into the *roux* and whisk smooth. As it thickens, keep adding more strained broth. Finally, add all the remaining contents of the pot to the roux. Add the Gosling's Black Seal

96

Rum, ketchup, Worcestershire sauce and vinegar and stir until thickened. Adjust seasoning with pepper and Tabasco. Serve hot over boiled rice.

Guy Fawkes Day

Strong evidence of the persistence of British traditions in Bermuda is the annual celebration of Guy Fawkes Day. You remember Guy. He was the one who would have seen Parliament in flames.

On November 5, 1605, four years before Bermuda was 'discovered' by the British, the "Gunpowder Plot" was uncovered. That day, the convening of Parliament would have found gathered King James and all government notables. In the cellars of the House of Parliament, casks of gunpowder were discovered and the treasonous attempt, pardon the expression, was defused.

To commemorate this day, every November 5, English expatriates, Bermudians and assorted revellers, historically lit bonfires, exploded fireworks and, in a show of gleeful barbarism, burned the miscreant Guy Fawkes in effigy.

Of course, certain fall-related dishes accompanied the event. In Bermuda, sweet potato pudding and cedarberry wine has been the tradition. Cedarberry wine, or beer, was made by fermenting the ripened berries of the indigenous

juniper that once forested the Island. These days there are far fewer cedar trees, and not many Bermudians would take the time to prepare so homey a potion.

Sweet Potato Pudding

In Bermuda, this is a pudding in name only. More like a spice cake, it has been said this treat was derived from *parkin*, an oatmeal and treacle cake well known to those from the north of England.

1²/₃ cups flour
1¹/₃ cups sugar
1 tsp baking soda
¹/₄ tsp baking powder
¹/₂ tsp salt
1 tsp ground cinnamon
¹/₂ tsp allspice
¹/₂ tsp cloves
¹/₂ cup unsalted butter
1 cup cooked, mashed sweet potato
¹/₃ cup orange juice
1 egg

Sift together the dry ingredients. In a mixer, blend together the butter, sweet potato and juice. Add the egg, then the flour-spice mixture, a little at a time until it is all well incorporated.

Pour the batter into a greased 8-inch-square cake pan and bake in a preheated 350-degree oven for 40 minutes, until the top springs back to the touch.

BERMUDA
TRADITIONS

Christmas

Christmas, as we know and celebrate it, began in the time of Queen Victoria. And although part of many a Christmas Day may include an amble on the beach, even a swim, a Bermuda Christmas still has an inescapable Dickensian aura. The shops all have wintry-looking displays of elves and fairies, of Mum and Dad by the fireplace. The palm tree-lined streets are festooned with lights, wreaths and banners, and there's a festive parade over which Father Christmas presides. In the often-balmy evenings, homes twinkle with coloured lights. And everyone has a Christmas tree: no longer the indigenous cedar tree, but an imported spruce or fir.

The Christmas Day feast in Bermuda combines several traditions. Turkey and ham, for sure, are on the table, but roast beef or goose—strong English traditions—are also alive and well. Whatever the menu, you'll also find cassava pie. This sweet-savoury dish is a combination of grated sweetened cassava root, layered with cooked pork and chicken, and baked to a golden-brown. Fruitcake and plum pudding are also part of a Bermuda Christmas. In Portuguese-Bermudian homes, *biscotos*, colourfully-iced ring cookies and cherry-laced pound cake belong to the dessert wonderland.

Boxing Day, an adopted British tradition, takes its name from church alms boxes opened on December 26, when the contents were distributed among the poor. Later, in the 18th century, the Christmas 'box' was used to share gifts and money with tradespeople and household servants. The tradition survives today in the form of cash gifts for the postman, paperboy and others.

In Bermuda, Boxing Day is celebrated by visiting friends' homes—and the drifting, rhythmic sounds of the Gombeys. Vibrantly-coloured, feathered and sequined Gombey troupes move throughout the parishes, dancing and swirling to insistent drumming, blowing on whistles and brandishing tomahawks. They inspire mystery, fear and joy as they go. They'll wind their way through the parishes again on New Year's Day and other special occasions throughout the year.

BERMUDA
TRADITIONS

The Classic Turkey

James I, who would not suffer pork at his royal table, is said to have popularised turkey in England. One year, I made turkey on the grill that was quite nice, but nothing says Christmas quite like a golden, aromatic bird at the centre of a festive table.

Traditional Chestnut Stuffing

1 lb peeled chestnuts
1 cup onion, minced
$1/2$ cup celery tops, minced
1 cup (2 sticks) unsalted butter
8 cups bread cubes (packaged is okay)
1 tbs fresh thyme
1 tbs or more freshly-rubbed sage
generous pinch of nutmeg
small bunch of parsley, minced
$1/2$ cup raisins, plumped in $1/4$ cup Gosling's Black Seal Rum
2 medium apples, peeled, chopped
1 tbs salt (or to taste)
$1^1/2$ tsp freshly ground pepper

In a pan of water, place the boiled, peeled chestnuts along with a small halved onion, and a little sugar and salt. Bring to a boil and simmer 35 minutes until tender. Drain, cool and chop.

For the stuffing: Sauté the onions in butter until translucent. Add the celery

BERMUDA
TRADITIONS

TURKEY TIMES·

A 10-pounder should feed eight normal appetites. Two smaller birds are better than one huge one if you're planning to feed more than 10 people. Why? You get a better balance of light and dark meat—four drumsticks to fight over. Besides, it will look pretty impressive when you bring them to the table. Always opt for more than you need; those leftover turkey sandwiches with cranberry relish or mayonnaise are heaven.

Start the oven at 450 degrees and after 10 minutes, lower the oven to 325. Turkey doneness test: when the thigh is pierced and the juices run clear, the bird is cooked. Instant-reading thermometer temperature: 185 degrees.

Weight	Unstuffed	Stuffed
8 lbs	2hrs 10mins	2hrs 50mins
10 lbs	2hrs 30mins	3hrs 20mins
12 lbs	3hrs	4hrs
16 lbs	4hrs	5hrs 20mins
22 lbs	5hrs 30mins	7hrs 30 mins

tops and cook another couple of minutes. Add the breadcubes 1 cup at a time, stirring well with each addition. Allow the cubes to sauté until golden. Transfer to a large earthenware bowl. Add thyme, sage, nutmeg, parsley, raisins, Gosling's Black

Seal Rum, apples, chestnuts, and salt and pepper and mix with your hands. Allow to cool completely. Stuffing may be prepared ahead. Do not stuff bird until just before it goes into the oven. See chart on previous page for cooking times.

To successfully peel a chestnut, make an 'x' on the shell with a sharp knife and either plunge them into boiling water for about 2 minutes, drain and cool, or roast them in the oven (400 degrees or over an open fire) until they split open. Peel away the hard shell and inner shell and proceed.

Holiday Smoked Ham

2 cups apple sauce
²/₃ cup brown sugar
¹/₃ cup Coleman's English Mustard
1 tbs ground cloves
2 tsp cornstarch
1 ham, bone-in

Score the ham by forming a grid across the fat. Mix together all the above except the cornstarch. Moisten the cornstarch with a little water, stir until smooth and add to the apple sauce mixture. Now rub down the ham with the mixture, making sure it gets in the crevices and clings all around. This may be done a few hours ahead, and the oven-ready ham kept refrigerated.

BERMUDA
TRADITIONS

Bake at 350 degrees for 1 hour, 25 minutes. The rub should form a nice, lightly-golden crust. Serve hot or at room temperature.

(This recipe is from educator and community leader, the late Reggie Ming, O.B.E., a great host and Devonshire Parish resident)

Standing Rib Roast

FOR 6–8
Served with Yorkshire Pudding and Stilton Peppercorn Sauce.

Still very much a Christmas favourite, especially with those who have a portrait of the Queen somewhere in the house. Buy the beef a few days ahead and dry-age in your refrigerator by setting the rib in a paper towel-lined pan. After 3–4 days, the rib will have lost a little weight, but the flavours will have become considerably more concentrated. If a dried crust develops on the ends, take off a thin slice and proceed.

FOR THE SAUCE
¹/₂ lb or more of Stilton cheese, softened
1 stick unsalted butter (room temperature)
¹/₂ cup Gosling's Black Seal Rum
2 tbs green peppercorns or mixed peppercorns
1 cup heavy cream
¹/₄ cup minced parsley

FOR THE YORKSHIRE PUDDING
2 eggs
½ cup milk
1 cup flour
1 tsp salt
½ cup water
2–3 tbs hot beef fat

FOR THE ROAST
10-lb standing rib roast, bones 'frenched'
(last 2 inches scraped clean)
4 cloves garlic, cut in slivers
4–5 tbs prepared Coleman's English Mustard
freshly ground black pepper

TO PREPARE THE BEEF
Tie the fat in place with butcher's string. Make little pockets in the beef with a small knife and secret pieces of garlic in each. Smear all over with the mustard and generously pepper the roast.

Preheat the oven to 500 degrees. Cover the bone ends with foil and place in a heavy roasting pan. Put meat in oven and lower the heat to 350 degrees and cook for 45 minutes. Cover the fat loosely with foil and cook another 75 minutes for rare (125 degrees on meat thermometer). Remove foil in last 10 minutes if more browning is desired. Let stand 5 minutes or so before slicing.

STILTON PEPPERCORN SAUCE
Make the sauce by creaming together the cheese and the butter until smooth.

Bring the Gosling's Black Seal Rum to a boil and add the peppercorns. Reduce the liquid until nearly evaporated, then add the cream and reduce by half. Lower the heat and slowly whisk in the cheese-butter mixture. Do not allow to boil. Whisk in the parsley and serve in a warmed gravy boat.

YORKSHIRE PUDDING
Beat together the eggs and the milk and whisk in the flour, salt and water. About 20 minutes before the roast is done, remove the beef fat from the roasting pan to a 10-inch skillet. Heat the skillet in the oven for about 10 minutes. Pour the prepared batter into the skillet and bake in the oven with the roast at 400 degrees for about 25 minutes until puffed and golden. If you happen to have 2 ovens, bake it in the separate oven. Don't forget to pre-heat.

Cassava Pie

There is no Christmas in Bermuda without cassava pie. Eaten like a potato or yam, the root of the cassava plant is a staple in many parts of the world. In Bermuda it is consumed primarily at the holidays in this weird-to-describe, but delicious-to-eat pie.

5 lbs grated cassava root (available frozen)
3 lbs chicken pieces, light and dark
2 lbs pork pieces

1 tin chicken broth, plus 2 cups water
3 cloves garlic, sliced in half
1 small onion, quartered
small bundle fresh thyme
salt and freshly ground pepper to taste

1 cup sugar (or more, according to taste)
¾ cup butter
freshly grated nutmeg to taste (1 tsp)
10 eggs
one 14-oz tin condensed milk
1 heaping tbs vegetable shortening
¼ cup flour
¼ lb (1 stick) of butter, melted

A day or two before you plan to actually make the pie, defrost and drain the cassava in an open bowl in the refrigerator. This will allow the root to remain tender and it also removes excess moisture.

Poach the chicken and pork pieces in the chicken broth and water along with the garlic, onion, fresh thyme, salt and pepper to taste, until just cooked. Drain, reserving the broth.

While this is going on, you can assemble the batter. In a mixer, cream together the butter, sugar and milk until fluffy. Now add the eggs one at a time. Season according to taste with grated nutmeg.

In a large earthenware bowl, blend well with your hands the egg-sugar mixture with the cassava.

Now liberally grease and lightly flour

an oblong pan (like a lasagna pan) with the vegetable shortening. This will ensure two things—that a nice crust develops along the sides and that you'll be able to get the pie out of the pan once it's baked.

Put down a layer of the 'batter' in the pan using a little more than half the batter. Put in a layer of the meats. Season again with salt and pepper if you like. Cover with the a layer of remaining batter.

Bake in a pre-heated 350-degree oven for 1 hour. Then cover with aluminum foil, lower the heat to 250 degrees and continue baking another 2 hours. Remove the foil. The pie should pull away from the sides when done. The moistness of the batter really determines the cooking time. Don't undercook; if you're not sure, test with a cake tester or knife—when it comes out clean, it's baked.

To ensure moistness, baste once or twice with the broth in which the chicken and pork has been cooked.

If more browning on top is required, simply run under the broiler for a couple of minutes. Brush with melted butter and serve, or cool and serve the following day. A little aging, as with many things, undoubtedly improves the flavour of this holiday specialty (many households freeze it weeks ahead of time, or even make a batch or

THE BRITISH STYLE

Although the British influence may be less obvious today than it once was, many Bermudians are proud to be British subjects. After all, it was the British who, however accidentally, settled Bermuda, and Britain which invested mightily with men and money in these small Islands. Britain shaped Bermuda traditions, style of government, even the look of the Island.

Bermuda became a colony in 1614, the first legal colony in the Empire. Self-governing from the very start, Bermuda is today the largest British Overseas Territory. There has been a Governor appointed by the Crown in Bermuda since 1684. Before that, the Governor was appointed by the Bermuda Company, a group of investors who sought to develop the Island for profit in the earliest days.

Forts and batteries were built on Bermuda from the beginning. In 1778, Bermuda became an outpost for the British Army to keep an eye on those American upstarts. By 1808, there were more than 1,000 soldiers here and Bermuda was seen as the 'Gibraltar of the West.' The following year, work began on the Royal Naval Dockyard on Ireland Island. In 1814, the attack on Washington was launched by the British from Bermuda. For a long time, trade with Great Britain predominated and until 1970, the currency of Bermuda was pounds, shillings and pence.

Beyond the earliest survival needs, the first cuisine was an attempt by British settlers to replicate what they knew best. Perhaps unfairly maligned, the British cuisine established here was, let's say, uncomplicated. "Our English nature cannot live by roots, by water, herbs or such beggary baggage," wrote one Elizabethan chronicler. "Give Englishmen meat...beef, mutton, veal, to cheer their courage."

Good old English dishes survive. Rib roast with Yorkshire pudding, fish and chips, steak and kidney pie, shepherd's pie, sweet potato pudding on Guy Fawkes Day, turkey or goose at Christmas, hot cross buns on Good Friday, and Anglo-Indian dishes like mulligatawny soup and chicken curry are all as unrelentingly British as the playing of *God Save The Queen* at official government events.

Recipes for all dishes mentioned—see Recipe index, Pages 129–132

BERMUDA
TRADITIONS

103

two extra for Good Friday celebrations). I love it cut in slices and fried in a little butter on Boxing Day.

Note: Farine pie in some homes is either the alternative pie or additional to cassava pie. Farine pie is often lighter and sweeter, and has vanilla extract, cinnamon, nutmeg, and allspice; otherwise the ingredients and method are identical. Some folks make one pie but use half farine and half cassava.

(This recipe is a subtle variation on the one taught to me by educator and community leader, the late Reggie Ming, O.B.E.)

Christmas Pudding

With Black Seal Rum Hard Sauce.

two 9-oz boxes of raisins
¹⁄₂ cup currants
¹⁄₂ lb mixed peel, cut in pieces
³⁄₄ lb fresh breadcrumbs (I use stale raisin bread)
³⁄₄ lb suet, finely chopped (this is essential—sorry, there's no substitute)
8 eggs, beaten
6 oz (at least) of Gosling's Black Seal Rum
additional Black Seal Rum to flambé

In a large earthenware bowl, mix together everything except the eggs and Black Seal Rum. Moisten the mixture with the eggs and then enough Black

Seal Rum so it will hold a shape. Press the pudding-to-be in a buttered pudding mould or basin, filling it full. Tie it tightly with a floured double layer of cheesecloth. Shaping it into a "cannonball" and steaming in a swaddling of cheesecloth takes the same amount of time as in a mould. Boil (steam) for 5–6 hours. Unwrap, turn out and serve steaming hot, with a sprig of holly stuck in the centre, and set alight by pouring flaming Gosling's Black Seal Rum over the top. Once the flames subside, slice into portions and serve with rum hard sauce alongside.

BLACK RUM HARD SAUCE
¹⁄₂ lb unsalted butter
3 heaping tbs sugar
pinch of salt
3–4 tbs Gosling's Black Seal Rum

Melt the butter and sugar together and add the rum, stirring until the sugar has dissolved completely and the sauce has begun to thicken. Allow to cool to hardness.

Traditional Fruitcake

The ancient Romans had a fruit and nut cake, called *satura*, soaked in honeyed wine. The word, meaning sweet and sour, is the basis for the word satire. Perhaps that's why this cake, long the victim of a love-hate

response, is so often satirised. In any case, you have to love a recipe that begins with a half-cup of rum, and ends with a cup!

1/2 cup Gosling's Black Seal Rum
1 tsp vanilla extract
2 1/2 cups mixed diced candied fruits
1 1/2 cups thinly-sliced pineapple
1 cup light sultanas
1 cup apricot preserves (thick)

1 cup hazelnuts, toasted, skins rubbed off and chopped
1 cup pecans
6 eggs
1 cup dark brown sugar
1 cup unsalted butter
2 cups flour
1/2 tsp freshly-grated nutmeg
1/2 tsp cloves
1 tsp cinnamon
1 cup or more Gosling's Black Seal Rum (for soaking)

Put the Black Seal Rum, vanilla, fruit and fruit preserves in a bowl and allow them to steep overnight in a cool place.

Next morning, pre-heat the oven to 300 degrees. Grease three 9 x 5 x 3-inch loaf pans. Add the nuts to the rum and fruit. Cream together the butter until fluffy and light. Add the spices. In another bowl, beat together the eggs and sugar until well thickened. Fold this into the flour mixture until well combined. Now pour it all into the fruit and nut mixture and fold until just combined.

Fill the pans two-thirds full and pat the batter down firmly. Now cover each pan with a layer of aluminum foil, sealing in the batter. Bake covered for about 2 hours, then 40 minutes uncovered, until the tops of the cakes have browned.

Allow to cool completely, then turn out of the pans. Sprinkle liberally with Black Seal Rum, before wrapping them in a Black Seal Rum-soaked length of cheesecloth, then in aluminum foil. Store in an airtight box, in a cool place, for 2 or more weeks before serving. You should re-moisten the cheesecloth with Gosling's Black Seal Rum as needed. Grape and orange juice may be substituted for a non-alcoholic version of this delectable holiday treat.

Sunday Breakfast
Codfish & Potatoes

FOR 6

It has been called the world's weirdest breakfast by the uninitiated, but it's no stranger than kippers or bagels and lox, to my reckoning.

Way back in 1512, when breaking the fast was just catching on, Lady Northumberland wrote in her household book: "First of all, they had bread in trenchers…a quart of beer and a quart of

wine, then two pieces of salt fish, six baconed herring, four white herrings and a dish of sprats." Obviously they were breakfasting on the forerunner of our Sunday fish breakfast. Artfully arranged, this makes for a pretty robust, soul-satisfying start to the day. A wild nasturtium on each plate is the perfect garnish.

2 lbs good-quality salt cod fillets
12 new potatoes
2–3 Bermuda avocados, ripe
2 lemons, quartered
6 Bermuda finger bananas or other small, ripe, sweet bananas
1/4 cup parsley, minced
egg sauce (see below)
tomato sauce (see below)

Soak the cod overnight, change water once. Make and have ready the sauces. Boil the potatoes until fork-tender. In another pot, cover the cod with fresh water and boil for about 8 minutes until the flesh begins to separate. Don't over-cook or the flavour will be boiled away.

While the potatoes and fish are cooking, peel, pit and thinly slice the avocado, rub each slice with lemon to prevent darkening, and arrange fan-like on each plate. Peel the bananas and put one on each plate. When ready, drain the fish and potatoes and divide among the plates. Serve with either or both sauces. Garnish with remaining lemon slices and sprinkle with parsley. Any leftover cod and potatoes should be used for Monday's codfish cakes (Page 94).

Egg Sauce

3 tbs butter
3 tbs olive oil
1 hard-boiled egg, chopped or mashed
1/2 tsp sherry peppers sauce

In a non-reactive saucepan, mix together the first 3 ingredients and bring to a boil. Remove from heat, stir in the sherry peppers sauce and serve.

Tomato Sauce

2 tbs good olive oil
1 Bermuda onion, halved, sliced thinly
one 28-oz can whole plum tomatoes, seeded, chopped
1 tbs fresh thyme
salt and freshly ground pepper to taste
1/2 tsp sherry peppers sauce

Sauté the onions in the olive oil until translucent. Add the tomatoes, thyme, salt and pepper and simmer 10 minutes or so. Add the sherry peppers sauce and serve. If serving only the tomato sauce, you may actually poach the cooked fish in the sauce a few minutes and serve sauce infused.

The Bermuda Wedding

Gold-Leafed Wedding Cakes and Cedar Seedlings

You're stuck in a line of traffic, wondering what the matter is. No horns are blown. In Bermuda, most folks only use their horn to say 'hi' to each other as they pass. After a while, the traffic will inch forward and you'll discover the cause of the delay: a flower- and ribbon-festooned horse and carriage transporting a smiling bride and groom from church. It's hard not to smile, no matter how long the wait has been or how hurried you are. The less-nostalgic arrange for a noiser mode of transport—a convoy of matching cars (borrowed from friends) decked out with crêpe paper ribbons and honking to herald the big event.

The idea of updating the traditional marriage has never really caught on here. Nearly as old as Bermuda itself is the marriage custom of gold and silver cakes, and the time-honoured tradition of planting cedar seedlings.

The single-tiered groom's cake—a plain pound cake encased in real gold leaf—is meant to symbolise the man's position as provider for the family, however quaint that may seem today. The three-tiered bride's cake is traditionally a fruit cake, with lots of ginger, symbolising the fruitful role of the wife as mother.

While the groom's little gilt pillbox cake is unadorned, the bride's has a tiny cedar seedling inserted on the top. The seedling is meant to be planted on the grounds where the newlyweds will make their home. As the tree grows strong, and is nurtured and prospers, so hopefully will the young couple.

The very top tier of the bride's cake is frozen and saved, to be enjoyed as part of the celebration for the first born (or the first anniversary, whichever is sooner). The second tier is shared between the parents and the third and largest is shared among the many guests. Huge weddings (Bermudians like large gatherings—600 is not uncommon) often necessitate an extra cake be made. This cake, or indeed the wedding cake, may be a multi-tiered, massively-frosted extravaganza. But the traditional wedding will at least have the two small cakes, bride's and groom's, for their symbolic value.

BERMUDA
TRADITIONS

Roof Wettings & Ship Christenings

A Bermudian roof wetting ceremony involves very few elements: the roof of a new building or home, the owner and builder who created it—and a bottle of Gosling's Black Seal Rum. I can only assume in shipbuilding days, it was rum, not champagne, used to christen Bermuda's finely crafted ships. Most builders of early homes in Bermuda were shipwrights first and foremost, as evidenced in the use of many shipbuilding techniques and designs, so why not treat a home like a sailing vessel? A prime example can be seen by visiting Old Devonshire Church.

Why the roof? As far as I can make out, the roof is really the most important part of a home in Bermuda. Besides being the 'crown' of the structure, it is, in many instances, the only source for water. Rain water is collected on local roofs, stored in tanks under the houses and pumped into homes for regular use.

When a new building goes up in Bermuda—from a small cottage to a big office block—a celebration is held. The owners, architect, and contractor scramble on to the roof and a dousing of Gosling's Black Seal Rum paves the way for numerous toasts.

English Afternoon Tea
Tea, Sandwiches & Tea Sweets

Tea, some historians conjecture, had been drunk as early as 2737 B.C. The royal yen for tea was brought to England by Charles II, when he returned from exile with his new Portuguese queen, Catherine de Braganza. That royals took tea did a great deal to popularise the beverage, but tea time as we know it was still a long way off. When, in 1660, diarist Samuel Pepys recorded his first sip, tea was most likely still slurped from a bowl in the manner of the Chinese.

The tea-taking tradition was created by Anna, Duchess of Bedford, who, while at her country estate, Castle Belvoir, disliked the faint, failing feeling she experienced everyday around five o'clock. To remedy this, she would invite a few friends to her boudoir to partake of tea and cakes. So revitalising were these occasions, once she returned to London, she held afternoon teas, to the delight of all invited. She must have been quite popular to have set off a trend that became a British ritual!

The ceremony of afternoon tea in Bermuda is perpetuated mostly in hotels, guest houses and restaurants.

BERMUDA TRADITIONS

FIVE STEPS TO BREWING A PERFECT POT

1. Use a clean, well-warmed pot (rinse with boiling water).
2. Put in one level teaspoon for each six-ounce cup desired, and one for the pot.
3. Bring cold water to a rolling boil and pour upon the leaves in the pot.
4. Cover quickly and allow to steep for four to five minutes for fullest flavour.
5. Stir once, recover, allow tea to settle and pour.

Tea may be accompanied by milk (not cream) sugar or lemon, although purists will look askance at their use. Milk is never taken with Oolong teas.

BERMUDA
TRADITIONS

Tea Sandwiches

Trim the crusts from some nice, firm, good quality white bread, home-made if you are so inclined (or have a bread machine). Coat every slice on one side with mixed equal parts of softened sweet butter and mayonnaise.

Between two pieces, place very thin slices of cucumber and sprinkle with a little sea salt. Between another two, put thinly-sliced onion or radish. Between yet another pair, layer fresh, bright green watercress. Shaved Virginia ham would also make a nice tea sandwich. Cut the large sandwiches into triangles or circles (eating the leftovers, of course!). Coat the edges with some of the butter-mayo mix and roll them in minced parsley.

A further variation using the same procedure might find cream cheese and chutney between the bread, or Elsenham's Patum Peperium (also called gentlemen's relish made with anchovies and butter) with thinly-sliced tomato, smoked salmon and minced dill, sliced egg and watercress. Experiment with sour cream and horseradish instead of butter and mayonnaise, coupling it with thinly-sliced roast beef, pork, or mustard mayonnaise with sliced turkey or chicken.

Richmond Maids of Honour

FOR THE SHORT CRUST
1½ cups unbleached flour
¼ tsp salt
2 tsp sugar
6 tbs unsalted butter, cut in pieces
2 tbs lard or shortening, cut in pieces
3–4 tbs iced water

Mix together all the dry ingredients. Cut butter and shortening into the dry ingredients with a fork or pastry cutter until the mixture resembles a coarse meal.

Add the iced water and mix until a ball is formed. Dust the ball with flour and chill an hour or more before rolling out. You can freeze the dough for future use.

FOR THE HONOURABLE MAIDS
3 egg yolks
½ cup sugar
¼ cup ground almonds
juice of a lemon
grated rind of a lemon
¼ cup heavy cream
pinch of nutmeg
your favourite fruit preserves to coat the maids' bottoms (dear me!)

Roll out the pastry to ¼-inch thickness and with a cookie-cutter, cut out 3-inch rounds. Press the rounds into well-greased muffin tins or tartlet pans, pressing to form low sides. Chill.

Beat together the egg yolks and sugar until thick and lemony. Add the almonds, lemon juice and rind and stir. Add the heavy cream and nutmeg and stir a few more times until smooth.

Take the lined muffin tins from the fridge and spread a little of the preserves in the bottom of each tart. Fill the tarts three-quarters full with the egg yolk mixture. Bake for 20 minutes in a preheated 350-degree oven until the filling is golden and just set. Allow to cool completely, then carefully extract from the tins. Serve with a dollop of whipped or clotted cream, and a dot of preserves on top.

Buttermilk Scones

2 cups all-purpose flour
1 tbs sugar
2 tsp baking powder
½ tsp baking soda
pinch of salt
6 tbs cold butter
½ cup plus 2 tbs buttermilk

Sift together all the dry ingredients. Cut the butter into the dry ingredients with a fork or pastry cutter until the mixture resembles a coarse meal.

BERMUDA TRADITIONS

Add ½ cup buttermilk and work into a ball of dough, using additional buttermilk as needed. Knead the dough briefly on a floured surface. Roll or pat into a large ½-inch-thick circle. Use a 2-inch-round cookie-cutter to punch out scones. Gather the scraps and roll out again, cut out scones until all the dough is used.

Bake the scones in a preheated 400-degree oven for about 12 minutes until they turn golden. Very nice served with warm Devonshire cream and raspberry preserves. Very nice, indeed.

KNOW YOUR TEAS

Tea should never be confused with tisanes or herbal infusions. Fine teas, that is the unbagged, loose-leaves of the tea bush, is what's preferred by the perspicacious tea taker.

DARJEELING Known as the 'champagne' of teas, this leaf from the Himalayan foothills is among the best-known and most commonly served. Say "tea" and you'll usually get Darjeeling.

ASSAM A strong and, brightly-coloured tea from Northern India. Widely enjoyed.

KEEMUN A black tea from China, with a delicate flavour, grown in the province of Anhui.

OOLONG Another China tea, large-leafed, with a flavour likened to ripe peaches.

ENGLISH BREAKFAST A blend of Ceylon and India teas, full-bodied and well suited to an early-morning first cup.

EARL GREY The tea purist might draw the line at this blend of China and Darjeeling teas that's fortified by oil of Bergamot. Very tasty just the same.

LAPSANG SOUCHUNG Grown in Fujian province in the south China, this pungent tea always reminds me of burning tyres.

CEYLON This aromatic tea is grown in the high elevations of Sri Lanka. Nice iced.

ROSE POUCHONG A China tea from Guandong province, scented with rose petals.

RUSSIAN CARAVAN Once brought overland to Russia by camel, Caravan tea is a blend of Tawian and China teas.

GREEN GUNPOWDER The curled leaves resemble lead shot, and the pale-coloured tea is never taken with milk, lemon or sugar.

CONSTANT COMMENT I like this 'feel-good' tea enlivened with orange peel, clove and spices. It's like drinking Christmas.

There are an increasing number of flavoured teas too numerous to mention. If you like these teas, you probably like flavoured coffees.

BERMUDA
TRADITIONS

111

Desserts

Cakes

Black Seal Rum Chocolate Black Cake

In the Caribbean, a black cake is a dark, gingery fruitcake. This version, however, is a fruity, rum and chocolate cake.

1 cup dates, chopped
1 tsp baking soda
3/4 cup boiling water
2 tsp Gosling's Black Seal Rum
1 tsp vanilla extract

1/2 lb unsalted butter
1 cup sugar
3 eggs

2 cups flour
1/2 cup cocoa
1 tsp baking soda
1/2 tsp salt
1/2 cup semi-sweet chocolate chips
1/2 cup brown sugar
1/2 cup pecans, chopped
1/2 cup Gosling's Black Seal Rum

FOR THE GARNISH
confectioner's sugar
1 pint or more fresh raspberries or berries of
your choice

Grease and flour a Bundt or tube pan. Mix together the pecans and brown sugar and sprinkle into the pan. Plunge the dates into the boiling water, remove from the heat and add the baking soda, Gosling's Black Seal Rum and vanilla. Allow to cool while you cream together the butter and sugar until light and fluffy. Add the eggs one at a time.

Mix together the flour, cocoa, baking soda and salt. Add this mixture and the date water mixture alternately into the butter and sugar, beating all the while. When all is incorporated, fold in the chocolate chips. Spoon the thick batter into the pan and bake in a pre-heated 350-degree oven for 1 hour or until the tester comes out clean.

Allow to cool at least 10 minutes before inverting on to a wire rack. While still warm, and upside down, give it a good dousing of Gosling's Black Seal Rum. Invert, allow to cool about 5 more minutes before attempting to ease off the pan. When completely cool, douse again with Gosling's Black Seal Rum. You may serve it now, or even better, refrigerate overnight or longer. Sprinkle with even more rum before serving. It should become fudge-like, not wet. Dust with powdered sugar 'snow' and fill the centre with fresh raspberries for a dramatic flourish.

DESSERTS

113

Loquat Cheesecake

In the early spring, loquats ripen on trees all over Bermuda. This fruit is somewhere between an apricot and a kumquat in size and flavour. Children snack on them, or use them as projectiles while waiting for the bus. Loquats find their way into pies, liqueur, up-side-down cakes, chutneys, jams and this cheesecake.

2 lbs cream cheese (4 boxes), at room temperature
1 cup sugar
4 eggs
¼ cup heavy cream
2 ounces Bermuda Gold Liqueur (loquat cordial or apricot brandy)
1 generous tsp vanilla extract
¾ cup loquats, chopped (tinned Roland brand are fine). You can substitute apricot preserves—but it really isn't the same. Reserve 6 loquats, halved, for decoration

FOR THE CRUST
¾ cup Graham cracker crumbs or crushed vanilla wafers
3–4 ounces unsalted butter, melted
¼ tsp each cinnamon, nutmeg, ginger

FOR THE TOPPING
½ cup (4 oz) sour cream, mixed with 1 tbs sugar
½ cup toasted coconut

Cream together the sugar and cream cheese. Add the eggs one at a time. Add the heavy cream. Add the Bermuda Gold and the vanilla extract. Finally, fold in the loquats or chopped preserves.

Prepare a 10-inch springform pan with a crumb crust made from mixing together the melted butter, crumbs and spices, and pressing into the bottom and slightly up the sides.

Pour the filling into the pan and bake at 325 degrees for about 2 hours, or until the tester comes out clean and the cake has turned gold around the edges.

Put a layer of sweetened sour cream on top while still warm. Cool completely, chill overnight in the fridge. Decorate with loquats and toasted coconut before presenting to 'oohs' and 'aahs.'

Piña Colada Cheesecake

2 lbs (4 boxes) cream cheese, at room temperature
1 cup sugar
4 eggs
4 tbs Gosling's Black Seal Rum
¼ cup Coco Lopez coconut cream
1 tsp vanilla extract
½ cup chopped pineapple, fresh or tinned

1 tbs brown sugar
$^{1}/_{2}$ cup crumbled lemon wafers
$^{1}/_{4}$ cup unsalted butter, melted

$^{1}/_{4}$ cup sour cream
1 tbs sugar
1 lime, notched and thinly sliced
$^{1}/_{2}$ cup coconut, toasted

In a mixer, cream together the cream cheese and sugar until smooth. Add the eggs one at a time. Add the Gosling's Black Seal Rum, Coco Lopez coconut cream and vanilla, mixing well. Finally, fold in the pineapple chunks.

Combine the butter, brown sugar and crushed lemon wafers and press into the bottom of a 10-inch springform pan. Pour creamed mixture into the pan and bake at 325 degrees for $1^{3}/_{4}$–2 hours. Top should be lightly golden and set. It may crack, but don't worry.

Mix together the sugar and sour cream. While the cheesecake is still hot, spread the top with the sweetened sour cream. Put back in the oven for 5 minutes to set the sour cream. Cool completely, chill for 2 hours or overnight. Decorate with notched wheels of lime and sprinkle with toasted coconut.

Loquat Upside Down Cake

2 cups loquats
1 cup light brown sugar
$^{1}/_{3}$ cup (5 tbs) butter

1 cup flour
1 tsp baking powder
3 eggs, separated
1 cup sugar
juice from cooked loquats

$^{1}/_{2}$ pint heavy cream, whipped stiff

Blanch the loquats in $^{1}/_{2}$ cup of water briefly and reserve half the water. Peel and pit them over the reserved water to catch the juice. Prepare a heavy iron skillet (10-inch) by melting the butter and sugar together and layering on the cooked loquats.

Beat the egg yolks with half the sugar until lemony and fluffy. Add the reserved loquat juice and beat well. Sift together the flour and baking powder and work it into the egg yolk mixture. Beat the egg whites with the remaining sugar to stiff peaks and fold into the yolk-flour mixture. Pour this batter into the skillet and bake 45 minutes in a 350-degree oven. Remove from the oven and allow to cool 5 minutes. Turn out of the pan and serve warm, topped with dollops of whipped cream.

DESSERTS

Cherry Nut Cake

A traditional Portuguese holiday treat. Great year round. You can double this recipe. Fun for gift-giving, too.

1 cup sugar
1/2 lb unsalted butter
6 medium eggs, separated
1 tsp vanilla extract
1/2 tsp lemon extract
1 tbs Gosling's Black Seal Rum
1 3/4 cup plus 2 tbs flour
1 lb glazed cherries, chopped
1 lb walnuts, chopped
brown paper or baker's parchment
additional 2 tbs Gosling's Black Seal Rum

In a mixer, cream together the butter and the sugar until light and fluffy. In a separate bowl, beat the egg yolks until pale and creamy. Add the vanilla, lemon and Gosling's Black Seal Rum. Beat this mixture into the butter and sugar mixture until well combined. Slowly beat in the flour a little at a time. Beat the egg white to stiff peaks and fold into the flour mixture. Toss the cherries and walnuts with a little flour to give them a dusting.

Grease and flour a standard loaf pan and line the bottom and sides with brown paper or baker's parchment. Put slightly less than half the batter in the pan. Sprinkle with a layer of cherries and walnuts. Top with remaining batter. Bake in a pre-heated 300-degree oven for up to 1 1/2 hours, or until the tester comes out clean. Cool 10 minutes before turning out on to wire racks to cool completely. Remove paper. Sprinkle with additional Gosling's Black Seal Rum.

(Adapted from a recipe by Beatrice Faries)

DESSERTS

RUM FACTS
The Daily Tot

In 1655, Britain captured Jamaica, a fine source of sugar, molasses and cocoa beans, from the Spaniards. Rum quickly became the official drink of the British Royal Navy, replacing beer that soured after a few weeks at sea. A twice-daily "tot," an eighth of a pint to be exact, was doled out by the ship's purser to every seaman. Although reduced in quantity by half in 1850, the tradition remained unbroken until 1970.

Sweet Potato, Rum & Walnut Pie

one 8-inch pie crust (see below, or bought)
2 hefty sweet potatoes, scrubbed
²/₃ cup brown sugar
1 tbs dark molasses
1 tsp cinnamon
1 tsp ginger or more to taste
¹/₂ tsp nutmeg
¹/₄ tsp cloves, ground
2 tbs Gosling's Black Seal Rum
3 eggs
1 cup heavy cream
pinch of salt
¹/₂ cup walnut pieces, 12 large walnut pieces
whipped cream for garnish

In a casserole, bake the sweet potatoes with a half cup of water at 350 degrees for 1¹/₂ hours. Cool, peel, cut in chunks. In a food processor, put the sweet potatoes with all the remaining ingredients, except the walnuts, and purée. Fold the walnuts into the purée and pour into an 8-inch pre-baked pie shell (see simple pie crust below). Smooth the top and bake at 450 degrees for 10 minutes. Lower the heat to 350 degrees and bake 30 minutes longer or until the tester comes out clean. Cool for at least a half-hour before serving, topped with dollops of whipped cream decorated with walnut halves or pieces.

DESSERTS

EXCELLENT SIMPLE PIE CRUST

1¹/₂ cups flour
¹/₄ tsp salt
¹/₄ lb (1 stick) unsalted butter cold, cut in pieces
1 tbs sugar
1 extra large egg yolk
2 tbs iced water

Mix together the flour and the salt. With a pastry cutter or fork, cut in the butter until the mixture resembles a coarse meal. Use your fingers to crumble the large bits. If you have hot hands, you'll melt the butter. Sprinkle in the sugar and blend with a few brief fork strokes. Mix the egg yolk in the iced water and pour into the flour mixture. Working quickly, and using a fork, fingers or both, combine the egg completely to form a dough. If it is too dry and crumbly, add a few drops of water. Put on a large sheet of waxed paper and press into a large roundish disk and chill 20 minutes or more before rolling out between two sheets of waxed paper and fitting to pie tin. Chill well before use.

To pre-bake a pie shell, line with a layer of waxed paper weighted down with rice, dried beans or baking weights (pellets)—which are meant to be cooled, saved and re-used. Bake for 10–15 minutes at 375 degrees. Cool and proceed.

Puddings & Breads

Arrowroot Pudding

Arrowroot was a major export for many years. The best is said to have come from St. David's Island. The remains of an arrowroot factory may be seen in the Botanical Gardens.

DESSERTS

3 tbs arrowroot
1 tbs cold water
2 cups whole milk, boiling
1 tbs butter
pinch of salt
1/2 tsp sugar
5 eggs, beaten well
1 tsp vanilla extract (or lemon extract)

Mix the arrowroot in the cold water. Whisk in the boiling milk and beat until smooth. Add the butter, salt, sugar and allow to cool. Add the beaten eggs, vanilla (or lemon). Pour into a large soufflé dish or individual custard cups, dust with grated nutmeg and bake in a 325-degree oven until set and golden on top.

Bermuda Bread Pudding

With Gosling's Black Seal Rum Sauce.

5 whole eggs
1 egg yolk
1/2 cup sugar
2 cups milk
1 cup heavy cream
1 tbs vanilla extract
4 tbs cinnamon
1/2 tsp nutmeg
8–10 slices of day-old Portuguese egg bread or other sweet bread (if you have fresh bread, dry it out in a 200-degree oven for at least 10 minutes)
1/4 stick butter
2 cups raisins, soaked in 1/4 cup Gosling's Black Seal Rum
rum sauce (recipe follows)

Beat the eggs and sugar until light and fluffy. Slowly add the milk and heavy cream, then lower the speed. Add vanilla, half the cinnamon and all the nutmeg.

Butter a deep 9-inch square pan and sprinkle the bottom with 2 teaspoons of cinnamon and 2/3 of a cup of raisins. Shingle a layer of bread over this and spoon on 1/3 of the custard mixture, pressing so it soaks in. Repeat this

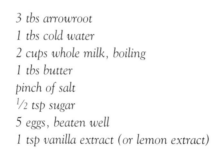

sequence of cinnamon, raisins, bread, custard once more, making sure the bread is well saturated with custard mixture. Sprinkle the top with additional cinnamon. Cover the pan with a lightly-buttered sheet of heavy-duty aluminum foil. Place the pan in a larger pan filled halfway up with hot water and bake at 300 degrees for 1 hour. Serve warm with Gosling's Black Seal Rum sauce.

FOR THE RUM SAUCE
3 eggs
1/2 lb (2 sticks) unsalted butter, melted
1 1/2 cups sugar
2 tsp Gosling's Black Seal Rum

In a mixer, on highest speed, whip eggs and sugar until thickened and smooth. Add melted butter in a drizzle and mix until cooled. Mix in Black Seal Rum until well blended. Keep at room temperature or chill and bring back to room temperature before serving.

Coconut Crème Caramel

FOR 12 SIX-OUNCE RAMEKINS
You can halve this recipe.

4 cups whole milk
2 tbs Gosling's Black Seal Rum
1 cup sugar
1/4 cup water

4 eggs
8 egg yolks
1 cup sugar
1/4 cup shredded sweetened coconut
banana slices and toasted coconut for garnish

Bring the milk to a boil, add the Black Seal Rum and scald 2 minutes. Allow to cool. Meanwhile prepare the moulds or ramekins. Boil the sugar and water until a light caramel colour is achieved (the darker the caramel, the more bitter). While this is happening, chill the ramekins. Pour a little of the caramel into each cold ramekin and swirl around to coat the entire interior with a film of caramel. Chill again if necessary.

Beat together the whole eggs, egg yolks and sugar until light and fluffy. Gradually add the scalded milk and stir until blended. Mix in the coconut. Pour the custard into the ramekins and set them in a roasting pan with 3 inches of hot water and bake in a pre-heated 325-degree oven for about 50 minutes, or until the knife comes out clean when inserted in the centre. Remember, the ones at the back will be done sooner, unless you reverse the pan two-thirds of the way there. Cool the custard in the ramekins. Remove from pan and chill until ready to serve. Before serving, dip in warm water, run a knife around the edge and unmould on to a plate. Serve garnished with slices of ripe banana and a sprinkle of toasted coconut.

DESSERTS

Dark 'n Stormy Frozen Soufflé

FOR 8

2 tbs candied ginger, finely chopped
3 tbs Gosling's Black Seal Rum
1 tsp vanilla extract
6 eggs, separated
1 cup sugar
1 tbs Bermuda honey (or other multi-floral honey)
1 cup heavy cream
cocoa powder for garnish

Soften the candied ginger in the Gosling's Black Seal Rum. Prepare eight 4-ounce soufflé moulds or ramekins by fastening a lightly-buttered collar of aluminum foil around each. Freeze the empty mould while you prepare the soufflé.

Whip the egg yolks with the honey and half the sugar in a double boiler until the sugar has dissolved and the mixture is light and fluffy. Allow to cool. Whip the heavy cream with the vanilla extract until firm. Whip the egg whites in an electric mixer about 10 minutes with the remaining sugar to stiff peaks. Fold the egg whites and cooled egg yolks together. Fold the egg yolk-egg white mixture and the candied ginger into the whipped cream. Ladle into the cold, prepared soufflé cups, filling three-quarters of the way up the collars, and freeze

DESSERTS

overnight. Gently remove collars before serving. Dust tops with cocoa powder.

(Created by Chef Marcus Wesch)

Three-Ginger Gingerbread

FOR 8

Bermudians love gingerbread at the holidays and year round. There are lots of recipes; this one is rich, dark and aromatic.

2¼ cups unbleached flour, sifted
½ tsp baking soda
½ tsp salt
½ tsp each of ground cloves, nutmeg and allspice
1 tsp cinnamon
2 tsp ground ginger
1 tsp freshly ginger root, grated or minced
2 tsp candied (crystalised) ginger, finely chopped
1 tsp cocoa
1 stick unsalted butter, melted and cooled
¾ cup sugar
¾ cup molasses
½ cup buttermilk
½ cup whole milk
1 large egg

Pre-heat oven to 350 degrees. Have ready a rectangular baking pan (11x7x2 inches) non-stick or greased and lightly dusted with flour.

In a bowl, mix together first 9 (dry) ingredients. In a mixer, beat together the butter and sugar until creamy. Add the molasses, buttermilk, milk and finally the egg. With the machine at its lowest speed, beat in the dry ingredients until a smooth and thick batter is achieved. Take care not to over-mix as this toughens the final result.

Immediately pour the batter into the pan and tap it on the counter to settle. Bake for 35–45 minutes until the sides pull away and the top is springy. Cool on a wire rack, invert or serve warm right from the pan. (Will keep wrapped in plastic for up to 5 days in refrigerator.) A dusting with confectioner's sugar dresses it up nicely.

Banana Bread

1¾ cups flour
½ tsp baking powder
½ tsp baking soda
½ tsp salt
½ cup butter at room temperature
1 cup sugar
2 eggs
3 bananas, very ripe, mashed
1 cup walnuts, chopped
3 tbs Gosling's Black Seal Rum
½ cup chocolate chips (optional)

Mix together the flour, baking powder, baking soda and salt. In a mixer, cream together the butter and sugar. Beat in the eggs, one at a time. Beat in the mashed bananas until blended. Now add the dry ingredients a little at a time until all is just incorporated. Fold in the walnuts, Gosling's Black Seal Rum and optional chocolate chips (I say optional,

DESSERTS

BANANAS IN PARADISE

Bananas are among the many crops which once grew abundantly, from pineapples to eddoes, citrus to tobacco—Bermuda's first currency. In 1633, the first bananas ever seen in England came from Bermuda and were, no doubt, proudly displayed by Thomas Johnson in his shop on Snow Hill, London. Today, bananas are still abundant. Small vest-pocket "plantations" and backyard plots yield several varieties of bananas, a relative to simple grasses, including cute finger bananas, small sweet strawberry bananas, plantains and red bananas. It's quite amazing to encounter the big pendant purplish pod that will soon peel itself open in delicate arab-esques to reveal tiny, pale-green talons that will mature into bright, irresistible bananas.

but I have yet to resist the option).

Pour batter into a greased 9x5x3-inch loaf pan, heart-shaped pan or whatever shape appeals to you that will allow the bread to come out at least 3 inches high. Bake in a pre-heated 350-degree oven for 1 hour, or until the tester comes out clean. Cool a few minutes, then turn out on a wire rack.

Portuguese Sweet Bread

2 pkgs active dry yeast
1 cup plus 1 tsp sugar
½ cup warm water
½ cup unsalted butter, softened
½ cup warm whole milk
4 eggs, beaten
1 tablespoon salt
4–5 cups flour
vegetable oil

DESSERTS

Mix together yeast, one teaspoon sugar and water and allow to bubble up. Beat together the sugar and butter, then add the milk. Add to the yeast mixture and combine completely. Now add 3 of the beaten eggs, the salt, and mix completely. While still in the bowl, add at least four cups of flour, 1 cup at a time, kneading as you go. When enough flour has been worked into the dough to form a somewhat smooth, elastic dough, turn on to a well-floured surface

and continue to knead the dough, adding flour to prevent sticking. Knead for a good 10 minutes. Shape into a ball and put in an oiled bowl and coat all sides of dough ball. Cover loosely with plastic wrap and allow to rise until double in bulk.

Divide dough into 2 balls and fit them to 2 non-stick or well-oiled skillets (for round), or standard loaf pans. Cover loosely and allow for the second rise until doubled in bulk.

Brush with the remaining egg and slit the top with a sharp knife just before baking at 350 degrees for 30 minutes, or until top is browned and shiny. Bread is completely baked when a hollow sound is made when you knock on the bottom.

With Fruit

Bermuda Syllabub

FOR 4

This old-fashioned dish dates from Tudor times and used to come in two versions—as a rich and creamy drink, or thick enough to spoon. Both brought together wine and cream. Popular well into Victorian days when fragile, delicately etched syllabub glasses were an essential household accoutrement. The origin of the name is shrouded in mystery. Some believe it to be a combination of old French (Sille is a region of Champagne) and Old English ("bub" is slang for a bubbling drink), or it may merely be a bit of jabberwocky.

4 tbs guava jelly
4 tbs port wine
1¼ cups heavy cream
6 tbs superfine sugar
freshly grated nutmeg

Mix the guava jelly and port together. Whip the cream into soft peaks, add the sugar and whip until stiff. Fold in the port and guava jelly. Pile into pretty glasses and chill, serve with tiny Johnny cakes (Page 65).

Black Seal-Poached Pears with Rum Sabayon

FOR 8

8 firm Bosc pears, peeled, stems on, cored, bottoms sliced flat
½ cup sugar
1 cup water
½ cups white wine
½ cup Gosling's Black Seal Rum
1 tsp vanilla extract
8–10 peppercorns
1–2 bay leaves

1 Constant Comment tea bag
1 stick of cinnamon

Place all but the pears in large pot and bring to a boil, then lower to simmer. Carefully stand the pears in the hot liquid. Poach for 25–35 minutes or until fork-tender. Let cool in liquid. They may be stored in this poaching liquid, and it may be used again with the addition of some water, or reduced to a syrup and served as a secondary sauce. Mmmm. Serve at room temperature, one pear per person and coat with cold rum sabayon.

FOR THE COLD RUM SABAYON
6 egg yolks
½ cup sugar
2 tbs warm water
¼ cup more or less Gosling's Black Seal Rum
1 pint heavy cream
1 tsp vanilla

In a double-boiler, beat the yolks and water briefly until frothy. Slowly add the sugar. Beat until the mixture begins to thicken nicely. Add the Gosling's Black Seal in a trickle. Beat well. When the consistency is like that of a medium-thick sauce, remove from heat. Allow to cool completely.

Meanwhile, beat the cream and vanilla into stiff peaks. Fold together with the cooled sabayon. Chill until

DESSERTS

ready to use. Spoon the sabayon over pears. Garnish with a mint sprig. Minimal, elegant.

Black Seal-Grilled Paradise Pineapple

FOR 4

1 large pineapple, quartered, leaves on
1 tbs unsalted butter
1/3 cup light brown sugar
1 tbs water
1/2 tsp cinnamon
pinch allspice
3 tbs Gosling's Black Seal Rum
the best vanilla ice-cream for garnish

Trim the core from the top of each of the four pineapple wedges. Cut the 'good' part of the pineapple from the shell in one long triangular wedge and remove. Place the empty shells on a foil-lined baking sheet. Wrap the leafy parts in foil.

Melt the butter and sugar together in a fairly large skillet. Add the water, cinnamon and allspice and bring to a boil. When the sugar has completely dissolved, add the Gosling's Black Seal and carefully ignite. Remove from the heat and let the flames die down. Put back on the heat and warm the pineapple wedges in the sauce, coating well (about 4–5 minutes). Fit the wedges back into the shells and slice into

inch-thick slices. Boil the sauce until quite syrupy and spoon over the pineapple. Now slide the baking sheet under the broiler for a few minutes until it bubbles and browns slightly. Carefully remove protective foil from leafy tops and serve immediately garnished with a generous dollop of vanilla ice-cream. Paradise re-gained.

Surinam Cherry Jam

The tart Surinam cherry, known elsewhere by its Portuguese name *pitanga*, came to Bermuda via Grenada. Portuguese explorers discovered the fruit in Central America and spread it throughout the Caribbean. In Bermuda, it is found as evergreen hedges which bear fruit twice a year.

4 cups ripened Surinam cherries, blossom end snipped, pit removed
4 cups sugar
1/4 cup water

Save some of the seeds and put in a cheesecloth bag and tie. Boil sugar, cherries and bagged stones over a moderate heat until jelled. Press through a strainer and fill sterile jars. Seal, label and date.

DESSERTS

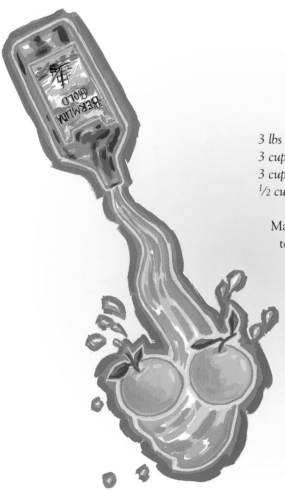

Bermuda Gold
Peaches

FOR 6

3 lbs ripe, but slightly firm peaches
3 cups of water
3 cups of sugar
1/2 cup or more Bermuda Gold Liqueur

Make a fairly thick syrup by boiling
together the sugar and water, brushing
down the sides with a pastry brush
dipped in water to prevent crystals
forming. When almost syrupy,
drop in the peaches and boil for
5 minutes until tender. Peel,
halve and pit the peaches and
place in sterilised jars and pour
in the syrup two-thirds to the
top. Add Bermuda Gold to fill.
Seal, label and date. Serve at
room temperature over the best
vanilla ice-cream you can find.

DESSERTS

125

Loquat Jam

Governor Reid was responsible for bringing this Japanese medlar plum to Bermuda in the mid-19th century. The jam is golden brown and irresistible.

6 cups of loquats, pitted (save some pits) and cut in half
6 cups sugar
1 cup water
1 cinnamon stick
½ cup Bermuda Gold Liqueur

Boil together the sugar, water, cinnamon stick, Bermuda Gold and fruit, along with a handful of pits for colour until thickened. Remove cinnamon stick and rub through a sieve and cool. Store in very clean jars. Seal, label and date. Keeps for two months in the refrigerator.

RUM FACTS

Post-Columbian Art

On his second journey, in 1493, Christopher Columbus brought sugarcane to the Caribbean. While sugar, in great demand in Europe, was the objective, rum turned out to be a delightful by-product. Refining cane produces molasses, which when mixed with water and allowed to ferment, can be distilled into a unique spirit—rum.

Cookies & Confections

Buscotos (Portuguese Holiday Cookies)

2½ lbs flour
1 tbs salt
½ cup sugar
4 heaping tbs baking powder
½ lb plus 1 tbs vegetable shortening
2 eggs
½ cup iced water

In a bowl, mix together the dry ingredients. With a fork or pastry knife, cut in the shortening until the mixture resembles a coarse meal. Beat the eggs in the ice water and add to the flour. Mixing quickly, form a dough. If it's too sticky, add a little more flour. Knead the dough for a couple of minutes until smooth. Set aside for an hour.

Make the buscotos by cutting off pieces of dough and rolling them into little logs a ½-inch thick and 4 inches long. Press the ends together to make a ring. Place on an ungreased, easy-release cookie sheet and bake in a pre-heated 400-degree oven for 10–15 minutes until slightly browned. When cooled, frost with red or green sugar icing. Keep the *buscotos* separate while the icing dries.

FOR THE SUGAR ICING
3 cups confectioner's sugar
¾ cup water (or less)
red and green food colouring

Make the icing by boiling together the sugar and water, stirring until it becomes somewhat glassy and makes a string when dropped from the spoon. If it's too thin, add more sugar. Colour the icing, half red and half green.

(Thanks to Beatrice Faries)

Old-time Coconut Cakes

More candy than cake, really.

2 cups sugar
2 cups brown sugar
2 cups grated unsweetened coconut
½ cup water
1 tsp ginger or more to taste
2 tbs Gosling's Black Seal Rum

In a heavy-bottomed pot, heat together the sugars and the water until sugar has dissolved and thickened.

Add the remaining ingredients. Cook slowly, stirring for about 20 minutes, or until quite thick. Test for doneness by dropping a rounded tablespoon's worth on a damp cutting board. If it hardens as it cools, it is done.

Glass Candy

An old Bermuda favourite with schoolkids.

3 cups sugar
½ cup water
1 tsp white vinegar
1 tsp butter
food colouring (red, yellow, green)
flavouring (lemon, lime, peppermint)
pinch of salt

In a heavy-bottomed pot, bring the sugar, water and vinegar to a medium boil. Stir carefully so all the sugar is dissolved. Brush down the sides with a pastry brush dipped in water if crystals begin to form. Cook for at least 20 minutes. Add the butter and cook for another 10 minutes until you reach the 'crack' stage on the candy thermometer (290 degrees). At this point, when a bit of the mixture is dropped into cold water, it instantly turns brittle.

Meanwhile prepare a muffin tin by greasing well with vegetable shortening. These will serve as your moulds.

Remove the molten candy from the stove and stir in the food colouring and

DESSERTS

127

flavouring of your choice. Now pour
⅛ to ¼ inch of candy into each
muffin cup. Cool completely. When
cooled, turn upside down and give a
few taps on the   bottom. Out should
pop the candies. Wrap each in waxed
paper, twisting the ends decoratively.

Black Seal Chocolate Rum Mousse

4 oz best semi-sweet chocolate
4 eggs, separated
4 oz (1 stick) unsalted butter
4 oz sugar
2 ounces Gosling's Black Seal Rum
whipped cream and white chocolate curls
for garnish (optional)

Melt together the butter, chocolate and
the Gosling's Black Seal Rum. Remove
from the heat. Beat the egg whites with
half the sugar until they stand in stiff
peaks. Beat the egg yolks with the
remaining sugar until they are light,
fluffy and lemony. Fold the still-warm
chocolate into the egg yolks. Carefully
fold this mixture into the egg whites,
preserving, as best you can the airy quality
of the whites. Portion into ramekins or
goblets and chill immediately.

   Garnish with a dollop of whipped
cream and shaved white chocolate
curls.

Dark 'n Stormy Ice-Cream

1 cup sugar
2 cups milk
2 cups heavy cream
8 large egg yolks
½ cup Gosling's Black Seal Rum
½ cup crystalised ginger, chopped fine

In a saucepan, combine the sugar, milk,
and cream, and scald the mixture over
moderate heat, stirring. In a large bowl,
beat the egg yolks until they are light
and thick and pour in the hot milk
mixture through a fine sieve in a
stream, and stirring constantly. Transfer
the custard to a saucepan and cook it
over moderate heat, stirring, until it
coats the back of a spoon. Transfer the
custard to a metal bowl set in a bowl of
ice and stir until it is cool. In a small,
stainless-steel or enamelled saucepan,
reduce the Gosling's Black Seal Rum
over moderately high heat by half,
taking care it does not ignite. Allow it
to cool. Stir the Gosling's Black Seal
Rum and the crystallised ginger into
the custard and chill the mixture,
covered, for 2 hours. Freeze the mixture
in an ice-cream maker according to the
manufacturer's instructions. Makes
about 1 quart.

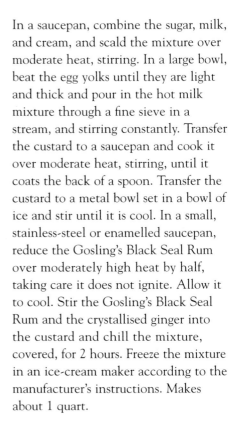

Recipe Index

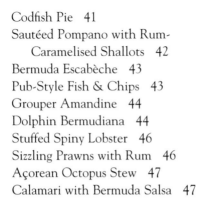

Sides, Salads & Sandwiches

RECIPE
INDEX

RECIPE
INDEX

131

RECIPE
INDEX